D0031075

How Safe is Nuclear Energy?

Sir Alan Cottrell, F.R.S.
formerly Chief Scientific Adviser to H. M. Government

HEINEMANN
LONDON · EXETER, NH

Published in Great Britain by
Heinemann Educational Books Ltd
22 Bedford Square, London WC1B 3HH

LONDON EDINBURGH MELBOURNE AUCKLAND
HONG KONG SINGAPORE KUALA LUMPUR NEW DELHI
IBADAN NAIROBI JOHANNESBURG
EXETER (NH) KINGSTON PORT OF SPAIN

Published in the U.S.A. by
Heinemann Educational Books Inc.
4 Front Street, Exeter, New Hampshire 03833

ISBN 0 435 54175 7

First published 1981

British Library Cataloguing in Publication Data

Cottrell, Alan
  How safe is nuclear energy?
  1. Atomic power – Social aspects
  I. Title
  303.4'83   TK9145

  ISBN 0-435-54175-7

Library of Congress

Catalog Card No. 81-81202

How Safe is Nuclear Energy?
Exeter, NH/London = Heinemann Educational Books
128 pp
8107   810319

Typeset by Red Lion Setters, London WC1
Printed and bound in Great Britain by
Richard Clay (The Chaucer Press) Ltd.,
Bungay, Suffolk

Preface

My aim in this book has been to provide the reader with a simple guide to nuclear safety; to lay the facts out, fairly and squarely, in a form in which I hope people can grasp them and then make up their minds about nuclear power in a more informed and sensible way than is possible at present. The book says almost nothing about the costs of nuclear power, the availability of uranium supplies, the general energy problem or the need for electricity. I believe that what matters to the general public is the safety of civil nuclear power and that in the end it is this, not any of these other factors, which will eventually decide the acceptability of nuclear power in western democratic society.

January 1981   A. H. C.

Contents

1

The fear of the unknown

Let there be light

A situation so full of fear and confusion that responsible members of the general public feel compelled to write of the 'malignant growth of nuclear power stations' is quite intolerable. The general public is entitled to something better than this. As a start, to clarification, enlightenment, facts and truth. And it is entitled, not just to selected facts which appear to support a particular point of view, but to all the facts, sweet and sour, delivered in a form which will enable people to make up their minds about nuclear safety and the merits and faults of civil nuclear power as compared with other forms or with the consequences of being without power.

Going on from this, if nuclear power is really unsafe, beyond redemption, then the sooner that everyone knows about this and rejects it, the better. Equally, if it is safe or can be made safe with reasonable effort, the public surely has a right to know this as soon as possible and to be relieved of the present miasma of fear. Yet again, if the real situation is actually more complicated, having some safe features and some unsafe ones, the public ought to be properly informed about this, plainly and truthfully, so that it may press for those particular features that will deliver to it the benefits of civil nuclear energy, safely without the dangers and worries.

It is hardly surprising that the general public is fearful of nuclear energy. For this is a new form of power for mankind, bringing with it the fear of the unknown. There are no centuries of familiarisation to guide our instinctive reactions to it. Moreover, it had a dreadfully explosive birth in the atomic bombs which destroyed Hiroshima and Nagasaki. Even in its most peaceful form it generates nuclear *radiations* which we cannot smell, see, taste or touch. In insidious silence these can produce medical effects of the kind most dreaded by people: cancer in the living body and genetic mutilation in future generations.

Nor is the general public alone in having these worries. Some leading and responsible nuclear scientists have expressed concern. Weinberg[1] described the development of civil nuclear power as a *Faustian bargain*, promising a virtually inexhaustible source of energy at the price to society of requiring enormous expertise, vigilance, attention to detail and social stability over many generations. Similarly, the Flowers Report[2] of 1976 came to the view that 'we should not rely for energy supply on a process that produces such a hazardous substance as plutonium unless there is no reasonable alternative'.

Civil nuclear power has also become one of the most controversial of political issues in western democracies. In Sweden the government was brought down a few years ago through differences over nuclear policy; and in the USA the government declared in 1977 that nuclear energy was the 'energy option of last resort'. National referenda on whether to go ahead with nuclear power have been held in some European countries and the efforts of opposition groups have virtually halted plans for nuclear power in Holland, Norway, Denmark, Austria and Italy. With the notable exception of France, nuclear programmes in other western countries have been delayed or scaled down so that, whereas a few years ago several of these were aiming to produce about half of their electricity from nuclear energy by the end of the century, today the targets are much lower than this in countries such as the USA, UK and West Germany.

It might be supposed from all this that there have been some terrible disasters caused by nuclear power plants, with great damage and loss of life. Furthermore, because people take disasters such as airliner crashes, dam bursts and large fires, in their stride—calling for no more than brief headlines in newspapers, a question in Parliament, and a routine tightening up of safety regulations—it might also be supposed that the incessant and intense public preoccupation with nuclear safety indicates that the nuclear disasters have been particularly horrific; perhaps towns wiped out and thousands killed. Nothing could be further from the truth. The safety record of the nuclear industry has been almost immaculate. So far, there has not been a single fatal accident involving radiation from a civil nuclear power reactor. There has been only one serious accident to any such reactor, that at Three Mile Island in the USA in 1979, but no member of the general public was injured physically by it. A large accidental contamination by radioactive waste appears to have occurred in the Cheliabinsk province of the USSR, in the winter of 1957–8, but opinion is that this was probably caused by a chemical explosion—not a nuclear one—at a store of wastes from a military plutonium factory.

The hard facts therefore are that nuclear energy has up till now been extremely safe. Then what is all the worry about? It is not about any actual harm but an apprehension about future possibilities. The public fears are imaginary in the sense that they are based, not on anything that has really happened, but what people have been led to believe *might* happen. In such a situation of fear of the unknown, everyone is surely entitled to have the facts presented to them, fully, fairly and clearly. Those who already have expert knowledge and real understanding of the technical and other issues involved surely have a responsibility to present the facts to the public—and its political representatives—and to explain their significance in as simple, straightforward, complete and balanced a manner as possible.

Neglect and abuse of public relations

The general public has not had such presentations, but has been let down by practically everyone concerned. It has been let down by the nuclear authorities who have been careless of their responsibilities for public enlightenment and who have alienated many people by their secretiveness, bland pronouncements and superior 'daddy knows best' attitudes. In Britain it has required the anger of some politicians, the insistent probing of some ministers, and the uninhibited cross-questioning of some public debates such as the Windscale enquiry of 1977, to get public relations taken seriously. In the meantime the nuclear authorities have lost much of the goodwill of the press, which they enjoyed in full measure in the 1950s and '60s, and are surprised now to find it quite hard to get a fair reporting. The position in the USA is perhaps even worse, where the accident at Three Mile Island has been a disaster in public relations for both the electricity company concerned and the governmental nuclear safety agency.

The public has also been let down by the nuclear scientists and engineers who have not tried hard enough to resolve, in a rational and scientific way, their own expert differences of opinion on key questions of nuclear safety. The basic principle of the scientific method—that of working towards an objectively based and freely agreed *consensus* of universally accepted knowledge—has been largely ignored in the professional nuclear debates. All too often the protagonists have staked out rigid positions beforehand, mustered up and manipulated whatever evidence they could to support these positions, and so become hermetically sealed in their separately congealed certainties. Little wonder that a senior civil servant recently felt compelled to complain that 'I have come to the conclusion that there is no such thing as a dispassionate viewpoint on nuclear energy'.

While judgment is bound to be clouded with passion about the political aspects of nuclear energy, there is no such excuse about nuclear safety, for the questions in this case are basically of a scientific and technical nature, the very kinds of questions that ought to be resolvable by the scientific method to the satisfaction of all professionals in the field. It is some disgrace for the scientific and engineering profession that this consensus has not been reached on nuclear safety, the more so as the primary issue—the biological effect of radiation—has been comprehensively studied and is now a well-ordered subject which can be discussed in a detailed and precise way. When the experts are so much at sixes and sevens and their disagreements are expressed so passionately, how can the general public be other than extremely uneasy about the whole subject and inclined to view every professional statement with suspicion? The general public has been let down here in two distinct ways. On the one side there have been some scientists who have obtained dramatic publicity by using, for example, the inevitable fluctuations of medical statistics, or minor day-to-day mishaps in the nuclear industry, as opportunities to deduce the existence of sensational and scarifying happenings which the industry is accused of concealing. On the other side there has been the tendency to keep silent about possible nuclear risks in case, through exaggeration and lack of perspective, these might unduly alarm the public. In any society, there is only one ethical course, which is to inform all the people, fully and honestly, all the time. In an open, democratic society this is also the only practical course, as Thomas Jefferson emphasised. The proper way is to put the whole issue, warts and all, fairly before the general public in an understandable form and to refute decisively, in public, all nonsense dressed up as 'science' by the sensation-mongers.

The general public has again been let down by those anti-nuclear campaigners who have exploited the public's ignorance of nuclear technicalities to aggravate its justifiable worries into unfathomable dreads and irrational hatreds; and let down by those television producers and feature writers who have presented their own slants and knockabout confrontations in place of honest, truthful enlightenment. The nuclear protesters have by various methods—ranging from public writing, speaking and action in courts of law and commissions of enquiry, down to headline-seeking marches and demonstrations, sometimes of a violent nature—succeeded in building up in the public's mind an image of nuclear operations as continually on the brink of catastrophe, so far avoided more by good luck than by planned security, and of nuclear energy as a general threat to the orderly working of society. They have further succeeded in influencing some governments into delaying, reducing and even halting, their plans for nuclear electricity.

About this book

In this emotionally overcharged situation is it possible, any longer, to give the general public a straight and objective account of the facts? Are we not all biased, one way or the other? Can we stop our own preferences creeping in and colouring the facts? It is really difficult, the more so because many of the key facts themselves are not absolutely hard and so leave room for contrasting interpretations. In this book I can simply try to steer what I hope is a fair course, but I ought to begin by declaring my position. I am in principle in favour of nuclear energy because I do not think that the coming multitudes can survive the bitter winds and sunless winters of the next century without it; and secondly because it is my view, based on the considerations set out in the chapters below, that nuclear energy *can* be made a sufficiently safe form of energy, certainly much safer than any realistic large-scale alternative.

Whether it *will* be safe in practice is an entirely different matter. It is a matter of making the right detailed choices from amongst the different alternative forms of nuclear power systems and practices that are available. These detailed choices all too often depend on sophisticated technical arguments about which the general public—including the governmental ministers who ultimately make the decisions—has to be largely guided by the experts. But it ought still to be possible for a well-informed general public to choose and insist upon those broad principles and strategies that will lead, with the guidance of the experts, to sound choices and safe practices. It is a fair hope that the technicalities themselves are not too abstruse for the public to grasp in a general way, sufficiently at least to enable them to recognise the real arguments and important points. This book is an attempt to make some contribution to this goal of a well-informed general public.

References

1 Alvin Weinberg, *Science*, 177, 27, July 1972.
2 *Sixth report of the Royal Commission on Environmental Pollution*, Chairman: Sir Brian (now Lord) Flowers, command 6618, HMSO, September 1976.

2

Unleashing the nucleus

Nuclear energy

Energy is bottled force. We keep it locked up, behind massive walls in hydroelectric dams, strong steel cylinders in engines, layers of insulation in electrical equipment and safety catches in guns. It is the very nature of force to break down resistance standing in its way, and smash itself forward. If the resistance collapses, the force is then out of control and rushes forward violently, throwing things about and wreaking havoc. But it can also be released gradually, against a carefully balanced resistance, always under control. When it is so tamed it can be directed to *work* for us, usefully; to move things about, lift them up, alter them in various ways, all at our own will. That is why the dictionary says that energy is the capacity for doing work.

The art and science of the power engineer is to obtain and provide mankind with sources of energy by locking up forces, safely, in such forms that they can be let out, under control, as and when they are wanted. But with any concentrated source of energy there is always some possibility, never quite zero however small the safety precautions can make it, of the bottled force breaking out in a sudden and disruptive manner. Dams break, buildings collapse, oil tankers explode, electrical equipment burns out, haystacks catch fire, boilers burst, bicycle tyres tear open, windscreens shatter, carving knives slip and frozen pipes split. We cannot avoid all such risks. They are part of life itself, for it is the energy of the world, the fluxes of natural forces, from which life is fashioned; and living, in its material sense, consists of manipulating the forces of nature, bottling them and releasing them to our advantage.

Nature keeps strong locks on many of its forces. The strength of rock keeps mountains standing up against the pull of gravity and holds high mountain lakes in place. The insulation of the earth's crust enables us to walk comfortably on the surface, despite the furious inner heat which occasionally manages to break out in volcanic eruptions. The basic laws of mechanics provide an exquisite, invisible, 'bottle' which holds the planets in stable orbits and stops them falling into the sun. Life itself depends on the locking up of chemical energy in special molecules such as sugars, fats, proteins and the genetic molecules of the double helix, known as DNA.

Some of nature's strongest forces are so securely locked up, on earth, that we were not even aware of their existence until this century. They are the *nuclear* forces, locked up in the *nucleus* at the heart of an atom.* All ordinary matter is made up of atoms, minute balls that cling together to form molecules. Atoms are extremely small. As a tennis ball is to the earth, in size, so is an atom to a tennis ball. Although so small to us, an atom is nevertheless big compared with its own constituent particles, its *electrons, protons* and *neutrons*, which are to the atom no more in size than are specks of dust to a tennis ball. The electrons fly about in the general space of the atom and define its overall size, but the protons and neutrons remain closely huddled together at its very centre, where they form its nucleus.

It is this huddling together, due to certain short-range nuclear forces, that is the lock which keeps energy bottled up in a nucleus. The energy itself comes from the protons, because these particles all repel one another intensely and so have a strong tendency to break out of their nuclear 'bottle' and fly apart, sometimes taking some of the neutrons with them. Protons and neutrons are very similar particles in many respects, but protons have the extra feature, which neutrons lack, of carrying an *electric charge*. This charge is the same for every proton—a positive charge—and the mutual repulsion of the protons is thus basically the elementary electrostatic effect that 'like charges repel one another'.

In most nuclei, however, the short-range nuclear forces provide a bottle strong enough to hold all the protons and neutrons together, despite the mutual repulsion of the protons. We owe our existence to the stability of this nuclear bottle, which gives permanence to the nuclei of the atoms from which we and most of our surroundings are made. But we also owe our existence to the eruptions and disruptions which occur in unstable nuclei, when the nuclear bottle gives way and allows energy and particles to escape. We stare straight into the face of a giant nuclear reactor, where these events take place, as we bask in the sunshine on the beach and enjoy the warmth, light and food which the sun's nuclear energy and radiation provide.

The science of nuclear physics has shown us ways in which we can unleash nuclear energy from *uranium* and a few other kinds of nuclei, here on earth. The requirements of civil nuclear energy, for making electricity, raise again the traditional problem of the power engineer: how to release this energy gradually, under control, as in a nuclear power reactor, rather than suddenly, uncontrollably and violently, as in an atomic bomb. This of course is one of the aspects of nuclear safety which we shall be considering. Nuclear energy however presents

---

* A glossary of special terms is given at the end of the book.

the power engineer with a new and additional problem. When a nuclear bottle is opened, the energy comes out in the form of high-speed particles and high-frequency electromagnetic waves, i.e. as *radiation*. It is thus impossible to have nuclear energy without nuclear radiation which, if allowed to reach people, can be highly dangerous to health.

The engineer thus has a second safety problem, that of holding back the radiation in a man-made 'bottle'—the containment structure of the nuclear reactor—which nevertheless allows the energy to come through. As we shall see, the radiation can be held back by various shielding materials, while the energy can be let through as ordinary heat. This is what is done in a nuclear power station. The nuclear energy is released and turned into heat in the central *core* of the reactor, where it is passed to a circulating liquid or gas—called the *coolant*—which absorbs the heat and carries it, along pipework, out through thick shielding walls of concrete and takes it on to heat exchangers and water boilers, from which steam under pressure emerges to drive the turbogenerators and so make electricity. The problems of nuclear radiation, in both their medical and engineering aspects, will take up most of the following chapters of this book.

Radioactivity

A nucleus can become unstable in several different ways. One of the simplest is that it may have excessive energy, so that its protons and neutrons move about energetically inside the nucleus, jostling each other and vibrating vigorously. In this case, the particles may relapse into a calmer state of motion by expelling their surplus energy out of the nucleus, in the form of a *gamma ray*. A gamma ray is a unit pulse of pure radiation, essentially the same as a pulse of light or radio waves but of much higher frequency and energy. Nuclear energies are usually measured as *MeV* (1 million electron-volts) and a single gamma pulse can typically carry about 1 MeV. This is roughly the amount of energy which the eye receives when we look at a bright star for one second. By our standards that is very small, but by atomic standards it is large. In a coal fire for example we would have to burn 250,000 carbon atoms to obtain 1 MeV of heat from them. The power of nuclear energy comes from the fact that we can get this much energy—and much more than this by the processes used in nuclear reactors—out of a *single* nucleus. When this single contribution is multiplied up by the immense multitudes of nuclei which may be doing the same thing, in an ordinary sized piece of the substance, the total energy output is very large.

A gamma pulse is one unit of high-energy electromagnetic radiation. An energy of 1 MeV, all concentrated in a single tiny gamma pulse, is particularly penetrating through matter when in this form. Thick shields of lead, concrete and steel are thus necessary to protect us from strong sources of gamma radiation.

Nuclei can also be unstable because they contain 'wrong' numbers of protons and neutrons—too many, or too few, or too much of an imbalance between the numbers of the two kinds. The science of chemistry starts with the protons, for it is the number of protons which decides to what chemical element the atom containing a given nucleus belongs. For example, every hydrogen atom has just a single proton in its nucleus; every iron atom has 26 and every uranium atom has 92. The *same* chemical atom—whether hydrogen, iron, uranium or any other of the elements—can exist in different variants, all with the same number of protons but with different numbers of neutrons. These variants are called *isotopes* of the chemical element in question. For example, the nucleus referred to as *uranium*−238 (i.e. with 92 protons and 146 neutrons, making 238 nuclear particles in all) is the common isotope of uranium. As we shall see, the most important isotope for nuclear energy is *uranium*−235 (143 neutrons). It is rather rare, because only seven atoms in 1,000 in natural uranium are of this kind.

Nuclei with the 'wrong' numbers of neutrons and protons often *transmute* into different nuclei, with better numbers, by *radioactively* emitting nuclear particles. They may in this way disintegrate either of their own accord or when stimulated to do so by a visiting nuclear particle. There are two common types of disintegration. First, the emission from the nucleus of an *alpha particle*, i.e. a *helium*−4 nucleus which consists of two neutrons and two protons, usually shot out at high speed, with a few MeV energy of motion. An example is the spontaneous transmutation of a *radium*−226 nucleus into *radon*−222 and an alpha particle. Some older types of luminous watches use radium as the source of the radioactive glow in the fluorescent paint on their dials. The second common type of radioactive decay is through the emission of a *beta particle*, i.e. an *electron* which is produced, either with a negative electrical charge, as a by-product of the conversion of a neutron into a proton in the nucleus, or with a positive charge through the conversion of a proton into a neutron. A beta particle generally leaves its nucleus at high speed, with an energy of motion in the range of an MeV or so. Modern watches use *tritium*, i.e. hydrogen−3, to illuminate their fluorescent dials through its beta decay into helium−3.

Because of their electrical charges, alpha and beta particles are easily stopped by matter, by means of its internal electrical fields. A sheet of paper is sufficient to stop alpha particles and the beta ones can be stopped by a sheet of perspex a few millimetres thick.

No-one can say when a given unstable nucleus will disintegrate spontaneously. There is no warning and no fixed lifetime before it happens. It occurs suddenly, out of the blue; a single, sharp event that seems to happen purely by chance. The only regular feature is the *half-life* of a large number of such nuclei. That of natural radium, for example, is about 1,600 years. This means that, if we start off today with, say, one million radium atoms, then in 1,600 years time there would still be about 500,000 of these as yet undecomposed. After a second 1,600 years, about 250,000 would still be left. After a third

1,600 years, the number would have dropped to about 125,000, and so on. During each 1,600 years about half of the nuclei 'die' but those that happen not to die remain, as it were, completely 'ageless' until they in turn chance to die.

Very broadly, and leaving aside many important factors that we will take up later, nuclei with half-lives on a timescale familiar to human beings—say from a few minutes to several years—are the most dangerous to health. This is because the very short-lived ones disintegrate before they can escape into the open environment, and the very long-lived ones are only weakly radioactive at any one instant. We shall look at this in more detail in Chapter 5. Since the strength of radioactivity depends on both the amount of substance causing it and on the half-life of this substance, we need some direct measure of radioactivity. This leads to one of the most important concepts that we shall need to use in this book, the *curie* unit of radioactivity. One curie is the intensity of radioactivity that is produced by 1 gramme of radium−226. More exactly, it amounts to 37,000,000,000 nuclear disintegrations per second. The natural radioactivity of the whole earth, due to its uranium and other nuclear contents, which is responsible for its internal heating, averages about 10,000 curies per cubic mile. The radium needle or tube used in the body for medical purposes usually contains about 0.005 curies, i.e. provides about 200 million nuclear disintegrations per second, whereas large medical machines for external irradiations contain up to a few thousand curies of gamma-emitting cobalt−60.

Nuclear fission

The master key for unlocking a nucleus and releasing its contents is the *neutron*. Normally, neutrons exist only within their parent nuclei but they do escape in one or two special types of nuclear disintegration. Their great importance as provokers of nuclear reactions comes from the fact that they carry no electrical charge and so are immune to the electrical forces by which atoms resist the approach of alpha and beta particles. Because of their electrical neutrality, neutrons can pass freely through millions of atoms, which appear mostly as empty space to them. If a neutron happens to run into a nucleus, during such a journey, it will often simply bounce off it, like a collision of billiard balls. Sometimes, however, a neutron may go right into a nucleus and become part of it. This stirs the nucleus up into an unstable state and may provoke it into making a radioactive change. For example, if a neutron enters a platinum nucleus it may cause it to transmute into a gold nucleus by casting out a beta particle, thereby (disappointingly) fulfilling the old dream of the alchemists.

The effect of neutrons on a few particular kinds of nuclei is far more drastic. This is because nuclei are rather like water drops in that they are globular and wobble to and fro in egglike shapes. When they are as large as the uranium nucleus they can even wobble into dumb-bell shapes, and occasionally go on from there to split into two distinct smaller nuclei, of slightly unequal sizes, together with a few neutrons thrown off. This spectacular event is *nuclear fission*. The gateway to nuclear power lies in the fact that the uranium−235 nucleus does this when it absorbs a neutron. The two nuclear fragments, formed from the opposite knobs of the dumb-bell, are thrown apart with great force, carrying an energy of motion of nearly 200 MeV. To produce the same energy in a coal fire, some 50 million carbon atoms would have to be burnt. As a result, 1 gramme of uranium−235 could provide nearly as much energy as three tons of coal. It is its extraordinary energy productiveness that places nuclear fission in an entirely new and different class from all previous methods, as a possible means of meeting mankind's future energy needs. In place of the daily streams of coal trains, bringing fuel to a fossil-fired power station, and the growing mountain of coal ash alongside the station, there is at a nuclear power station merely an infrequent truck, bringing or taking away nuclear fuel.

Because of the positive electrical charges of their protons, the fission fragments do not penetrate far into surrounding matter. They are quickly brought to rest and then acquire some electrons from the surroundings to become *fission product* atoms of chemical elements, such as strontium and xenon, in the middle range of nuclear sizes. As they are brought to rest, their energy is immediately turned into the heat from which a nuclear station derives its power. They are mostly unstable nuclei and generally undergo spontaneous changes at various times after fission. Their radioactivity is sometimes useful for practical applications, for example as in the case of caesium−137 used for medical and industrial radiology; but mainly it is a nuisance because in a large power reactor it eventually builds up to a very high level, e.g. 10,000 million curies, and elaborate precautions have to be taken to protect people from its radiations.

As well as releasing energy, fission products and radioactivity, the fission process also releases the seeds for its own continuation, in the form of free neutrons which fly off and can find their way into other uranium nuclei to repeat the process. When a uranium−235 nucleus splits, it throws off two or three neutrons with energies of motion of an MeV or more. Because of their high speeds, about 10,000 miles per second, these are called *fast neutrons*. Since more neutrons come out of a fission than went into it, there is a multiplication of free neutrons and hence an increased opportunity for further fissions to take place, through the 'burning-up' of other fissile nuclei by these released neutrons. A large-scale release of nuclear energy by a multiplying chain of fission reactions is then possible.

However, many neutrons get lost. Some escape through the neighbouring uranium into the general surroundings. Some get absorbed by non-fissile nuclei such as uranium−238, as well as by those of other materials used in a reactor core. The escape losses are minimised when the fissile material is in a large, bulky mass, so that a neutron has to pass through much material—and so is likely to encounter a fissile nucleus—before it reaches the surface and escapes. But even if we put together a great lump of natural uranium and surround it with a *reflector* substance that sends some of the escaping neutrons back in again, there could still not be a self-sustaining chain reaction, because the abundant uranium−238 nuclei would capture too many of the neutrons and then transmute into *plutonium* nuclei instead of undergoing fission. Something more is needed before this pile of uranium can become a working nuclear reactor.

There are two possible ways of achieving this: *enrichment* and *moderation*.

In *enrichment*, the aim is to increase the amount of uranium−235 (or some other fissile material, such as plutonium) in the fuel, so as to give the neutrons a good chance of meeting fissile nuclei rather than getting lost or captured without fission. Enrichment by separating the 235 from the 238, in natural uranium, is not easy because there are no chemical differences between these two isotopes to work on; but physical methods of separation have been developed, based mainly on processes known as *diffusion* and *centrifuging*. Separation into nearly pure uranium−235 opens the way to the uranium *atomic bomb*, but slight enrichment to a few percent of uranium−235 in 238 is sufficient to provide a suitable fuel for most power reactors.

The *moderation* method is more subtle but widely used. The principle is that, if a neutron can be slowed down until it is going no faster than an ordinary gas molecule, about one mile a second, i.e. it has become a *thermal neutron*, it is then less likely to be absorbed by a non-fissile nucleus and more likely to induce fission in a uranium−235 nucleus. The way to slow it down is to let it roam around for a while in a mass of non-absorbing substance, called a *moderator*, where it can bounce to and fro off many nuclei and so gradually lose most of its energy of motion. As well as not absorbing many neutrons, the nuclei of a moderator need to be fairly lightweight, so that they can rebound well and take up a lot of the energy when neutrons bounce off them. Three types of moderator are mainly used: light water, heavy water and graphite. Light water is ordinary water. It slows down the neutrons well but is also fairly absorptive and so is successful only if the uranium is slightly enriched. In heavy water the single proton of the hydrogen nucleus has a neutron attached to it, so forming the heavy isotope, hydrogen−2, called *deuterium*. It is the least absorptive of the moderators. As a consequence, heavy-water reactors such as the Canadian Candu type run well on natural uranium fuel. Large graphite-moderated reactors will also run on natural uranium, although there are some advantages in using slightly enriched fuel (e.g. 2% uranium−235). Light-water reactors use 3% to 4% enrichment.

Thermal reactors

We come then to the main types of thermal reactor now in commercial use for making electricity. The fuel, usually in the form of uranium oxide pellets, is sealed in stainless steel or zirconium tubes, which are called *fuel elements, rods* or *stringers*. These are lined up, end to end, in a large number of tubular channels which run in parallel through the moderator. The coolant, either water or carbon dioxide gas, is passed along these fuel elements under high pressure. In the **Candu** reactor the heavy water coolant and moderator is held in zirconium pressure tubes which enclose the fuel channels. In the **pressurised water reactor** (PWR) and the **boiling water reactor** (BWR) the coolant and moderator is light water, contained in a large thick-walled steel pressure vessel that surrounds the whole reactor core. The graphite-moderated **advanced gas-cooled reactor** (AGR) uses carbon dioxide coolant and the core is set inside a large reinforced-concrete pressure vessel. A list of various types of reactor is given at the end of this chapter.

In every case the coolant is led into and out of the reactor core by pipework, and there are other pipes into the core for inserting *control rods* and also, in some reactors, the fuel elements. The control rods keep the nuclear chain reaction at the required level of steady activity by absorbing excess neutrons, usually in boron which is a strong absorber.

During its period of up to a few years in a power reactor, a fuel element loses much of its original stock of fissile nuclei by burn-up, and at the same time accumulates a large stock of neutron-absorbing nuclear products. Because of these changes it can eventually no longer play its part properly in the chain reaction, and has then to be removed from the reactor as a 'spent' fuel element. When first removed, immediately after active service, it is fiercely radioactive (e.g. a million curies) and so is stored for a period in deep water to enable its radioactivity to cool off. After this, it may then be taken away to be treated in a *reprocessing plant*, where it is broken down in chemical solvents and separated out into uranium, plutonium and fission product waste.

Other types of reactor

As well as uranium−235 there are a few other easily fissionable isotopes. The most important is *plutonium*−239, formed by the transmutation of a uranium−238 nucleus after it has absorbed a neutron. This is a bonus in a power reactor which to some extent compensates for the loss of neutrons by absorption in uranium−238, in that it provides new fissile material to replace some of that which has been consumed. In power reactors the fuel elements are left in long enough for the burn-up of this plutonium to play a big part in the total energy output. In the *thermal* type of power reactor, however, the number of fissile nuclei created is less than the number consumed in fission, so that this *breeding process is not self-supporting*.

The problem is overcome in another type of reactor, the **fast breeder reactor** (FBR). If the fissile component of a reactor fuel is enriched up to about 20%, a moderator is then no longer necessary. The reactor can be run on *fast* neutrons alone. Hence its name, fast reactor. Furthermore, especially if plutonium is used as the fissile component, a larger number of neutrons then becomes available for breeding new fuel. This opens the way to the spectacular FBR which can, by transmuting uranium−238 to plutonium, create *more* fissile fuel than it consumes.

The most highly developed reactor of this type is the **liquid metal cooled** FBR (LMFBR). Its core is not much larger than a domestic water tank, but the coolant which is pumped through it at high speed is *liquid sodium*, an exceptionally good medium for removing the intense heat generated in this highly concentrated core. The fuel itself, in stainless steel cans, is a mixture of uranium and plutonium oxides, in the proportion of about 4 to 1. Up to a fifth more plutonium is created, largely in a region outside the core called the *blanket*, than is consumed by fission. There is thus the economically exciting prospect of being able in this way to use the common uranium−238 isotope as a nuclear fuel, through its conversion to plutonium. This would enable such vast amounts of energy to be produced from even the poorest sources of natural uranium—which exist abundantly everywhere, even in sea water—that the world's energy needs could in principle be met in this way virtually for ever. No pressure containment is needed for the LMFBR, because the sodium is a liquid at ordinary atmospheric pressure up to temperatures well above that of the reactor core. The hot sodium passes out from the core to a heat exchanger where it gives its heat to a second, external, sodium circuit. This in turn passes out to an outer heat exchanger which makes steam for the electrical turbines.

A possibility for the future, not yet completely developed, which works on entirely different principles, is the **fusion reactor**. This is based on *thermonuclear* processes similar to those that produce the sun's power, i.e. the fusing together of certain nuclei, particularly the deuterium and tritium isotopes of hydrogen, to form helium nuclei with a powerful release of energy. The main technical problems arise from the exceptionally high temperatures (e.g. 100,000,000°C) needed to promote the thermonuclear reactions. If it is successful, the fusion reactor will have two advantages. First, it can run on deuterium fuel, which is obtainable in almost inexhaustible amounts from seawater. Second, it is likely to present few safety problems, because it would use and produce relatively small amounts of radioactive substances.

A nuclear reactor is not an atomic bomb

To keep a steady chain reaction going, in a fission reactor, the average fission event must release just enough neutrons to replace the one that triggered it and also to compensate for the losses from non-fissile absorption and escape. It then happens that, through each cycle of events, every fission leads to exactly one more fission and the chain reaction is exactly self-sustaining, no more, no less. The reactor is said to be *critical* when the *multiplication* of fission events, from cycle to cycle, is exactly unity. When the multiplication is less than one, the reaction dies out as the population of neutrons gradually declines. When the multiplication is greater than one, the population of neutrons and number of fissions both grow, like compound interest (exponential growth), and the chain reaction is said to be *divergent*. This condition is deliberately aimed for in an atomic bomb, but is equally deliberately avoided in a nuclear reactor.

Neutrons move so fast that, in principle, they can set off a huge multiplying avalanche of fission events in a flash, certainly much too quickly for mechanical adjustments of the neutron-absorbing control rods to be made in time to bring such an explosively sudden release of energy under control. For nuclear reactors, however, the position is transformed through the fact that not all of the neutrons are immediately released from fission. Most of them (called *prompt neutrons*) are so released, but about one percent (called *delayed neutrons*) are held back, for times of up to a minute or more in extreme cases. This difference between prompt and delayed neutrons is of the utmost importance for the stable and safe running of reactors. We shall discuss it further in Chapter 8.

In complete contrast to an atomic bomb, which is designed to be highly divergent on prompt neutrons, a nuclear reactor is held down in the range where its chain reaction would always die out if serviced by prompt neutrons alone. Only when all the delayed neutrons also make their full contribution does the reactor become marginally critical. The art of running a stable reactor is thus to adjust the balance between the release and absorption of neutrons so that the chain reaction becomes just self-sustaining when all neutrons, prompt and delayed, contribute. Because the reaction then depends on the delayed neutrons, its *intensity* can change only slowly, giving plenty of time for the mechanical adjustment of the control rods. There is thus a safe gap between the level of *reactivity* used for stable running and that higher threshold (the *prompt critical* state) at which a divergent chain reaction based purely on prompt neutrons can begin.

In a thermal reactor there is an additional feature which distinguishes it from an atomic bomb. Its neutrons cannot sustain a chain reaction unless they are *moderated*. The rapid propagation of fissions, characteristic of the bomb, is quite impossible when the freshly-made neutrons have first to disappear into the moderator, bounce about inside it for a while to lose their energy, and then come back out again to find their way into the fuel as thermal neutrons; all of this before they can continue the cycle of fission events. The process of the atomic bomb—a divergent chain reaction produced by fast prompt neutrons—is thus impossible in a thermal reactor.

For the fast reactor there is also a safe gap between the stable running and prompt critical states. However, because this reactor works with fast neutrons, the additional condition that only moderated neutrons will sustain the reaction no longer applies. Nevertheless, the proportion of fissionable nuclei in the reactor (about 20%) is much lower than that in a bomb (over 90%) and the large amount of uranium−238 present provides an important protective feature against any approach to the prompt critical state. This is because it absorbs more neutrons when it becomes hot and so reduces the nuclear reactivity. In fact, if the sodium temperature of an LMFBR rises by 25°C, when the reactor is fully running, the power output of the reactor drops by one-sixth. The presence of large amounts of uranium−238 in a fast reactor thus provides a strong stabilising influence which is absent in an atomic bomb.

List of reactor types

Advanced gas-cooled reactor (AGR)
Thermal
Enriched uranium oxide fuel
Stainless steel can
Graphite moderator
Carbon dioxide coolant
Reinforced-concrete pressure vessel

Boiling water reactor (BWR)
Thermal
Enriched uranium oxide fuel
Zirconium can
Light water moderator and coolant (boiling)
Steel pressure vessel

Breeder reactor: see LMFBR

Candu reactor
Thermal
Natural uranium oxide fuel
Zirconium can
Heavy water moderator and coolant
Zirconium pressure tubes

Fast breeder reactor: see LMFBR

Fast reactor: see LMFBR

Gas-cooled reactor: see AGR, HTR, Magnox

Gas-graphite reactor: see AGR, HTR, Magnox

Graphite-moderated reactor: see AGR, HTR, Magnox

Heavy water reactor: see CANDU, SGHWR

High temperature reactor (HTR)
  Thermal
  Enriched uranium carbide fuel
  Silicon carbide can
  Graphite moderator
  Helium coolant
  Reinforced-concrete pressure vessel

Light water reactor: see BWR, PWR

Liquid metal fast breeder reactor (LMFBR)
  Fast
  Mixed uranium oxide and plutonium oxide fuel
  Stainless steel can
  Liquid sodium coolant

Magnox reactor
  Thermal
  Natural uranium metal fuel
  Magnesium can
  Graphite moderator
  Carbon dioxide coolant
  Steel or reinforced-concrete pressure vessel

Power reactor
  A reactor designed for producing electrical power, in contrast to a
  military production reactor (plutonium producer) or a research
  reactor

Pressurised water reactor (PWR)
  Thermal
  Enriched uranium oxide fuel
  Zirconium can
  Light water moderator and coolant (liquid)
  Steel pressure vessel

Steam generating heavy water reactor (SGHWR)
  Thermal
  Enriched uranium oxide fuel
  Zirconium can
  Heavy water moderator
  Light water coolant (boiling)
  Zirconium pressure tubes

Thermal reactor: see AGR, BWR, CANDU, HTR, Magnox, PWR and
SGHWR

3

How radiation affects us

The molecular basis

Nature has given mankind great powers. But power can bring good or evil; and nature leaves the choice to us. We now have power to produce atomic radiation in vast amounts. Many thousands of lives have already been saved by such radiation; and many thousands were also destroyed by it at Hiroshima. Atomic radiation, which can cure cancer, can also cause cancer; and ironically the same fundamental processes are responsible for both cause and cure. For nature has given us, in such radiation, a most subtly penetrating scalpel which can enter the heart of a living cell and there do surgery on the finest, most intricate, scale; on single biological molecules. The choice is ours, whether we use this power well or ill.

The story of how radiation affects us starts once more with the atom; this time however, not with its nucleus, but with its behaviour in chemical *molecules*. Each one of us is a huge collection of atoms—mostly carbon, hydrogen, oxygen and nitrogen—clustered together in molecules of various types, looking something like groups of frog-spawn. By far the most common molecule is that of ordinary water, our main bodily substance; but carried in this fluid are huge numbers of a great variety of other molecules—sugars, fats, proteins and the molecule of the genetic code (DNA)—some of which are extremely complex and made up of hundreds, or in a few cases even millions, of atoms. An atom in a molecule sticks to its neighbours, like frog-spawn, because those of its electrons which patrol its boundary regions can cross over a little way into the boundary territories of these neighbours and thereby partly belong to them. Thus are the atoms 'bonded' together by a common sharing of their outermost electrons. Radiation affects us by dislodging some of the electrons holding the atoms together in our bodies. A familiar example is sunburn. A single pulse of ultra-violet sunlight carries an energy of only about 5 electron-volts (i.e. 200,000 times smaller than the energy of a 1 MeV gamma ray pulse), yet a sustained bombardment by such pulses during sunbathing can dislodge many bonding electrons and so break up their parent molecules in our skin sufficiently to produce the well-known effects of sunburn. This shows that the bonding electrons are, by nuclear standards, only weakly held in place in their atoms and molecules, since low-energy pulses are able to dislodge them.

High-speed nuclear particles and gamma rays (and also X-rays, which are the same as gamma rays but differently produced) can in fact easily knock such electrons right out of their atoms and drive them far away. This process is called *ionisation* and it turns electrically neutral atoms into *charged ions*. For example, an atom which loses one of its bonding electrons (negatively charged) then becomes a *positive ion*. Conversely, when this expelled electron, in its wanderings through the neighbouring material, happens to attach itself to some other atom, originally neutral, that atom becomes negatively charged, i.e. a *negative ion*. Often, an atom remains in such an ionised state only briefly. The electron 'hole' in a positive ion may soon be filled up by another wandering electron; and a negative ion may easily lose a supernumary electron. Such processes of repairing ionisation 'damage' occur totally and almost instantly in metals, where all the atoms are constantly 'bathed' in a 'sea' of mobile electrons. But in organic substances and living tissue the damage is more long-lasting and can lead to the breaking-up of molecules, either directly through the weakening of key bonds by the loss of electrons, or indirectly through the chemical attack of other molecules and molecular fragments already disrupted by the radiation. The chemically disturbed ends of these fragments may attach themselves to the first molecule they meet and so form, with it, entirely new molecular combinations.

These processes of molecular break-up and rearrangement are the basic means by which ionising radiations bring about biological effects. In many cases, however, a living cell is unharmed by such changes, for most kinds of molecules exist in such large numbers within the cell that the loss or alteration of a few of them is of little consequence. A living cell also has vast resources for repairing or by-passing damaged components. The danger is when a rare molecule, critical to the functioning of the cell, is damaged. The most important example of this is the DNA molecule, the long thread of which carries the genetic blueprint for the reproduction of such cells. Damage here can lead to the death of the cell, or the inability to divide and multiply, or to the transmission of genetic abnormalities into future generations.

From the individual cell's point of view the crucial loss is that of its *proliferative capacity*, i.e. ability to reproduce itself by dividing into 'daughter' cells. Where a cell depends on this division for its place in the body, such a cell in effect 'dies' when it loses this capacity. It follows that cells which are in process of rapid growth and division are most sensitive to radiation damage. This fact is helpful in the treatment of cancer by radiation, since cancerous cells multiply rapidly and radiation therapy can stop them doing this. But it also means that an embryo or young infant is particularly vulnerable to radiation, and further that all those cell systems in the body which depend on rapid multiplication are similarly vulnerable. This applies for example to bone marrow in which blood cells are made, as well as to the basal layer of the skin, the lining of the intestine and the male reproductive cells. Thus anaemia and sterility can result from severe doses of radiation. In the fully grown adult, the continual multiplication of many types of cells ceases, as a result of normal biological control. In such cases these cells often show a considerable biological insensitivity to radiation. On the other hand, radiation can in some tissues bring about a loss of this biological control and a cancerous multiplication of the uncontrolled cells can then begin.

How much radiation?

Radiation biology is obviously an immensely complicated subject. The first step in getting an overall grasp of it is to have some simple and general, but trustworthy, measure of what we mean by a *dose* of radiation. There are two such measures. The starting point for both is the *amount of energy* deposited from the radiation by ionisation in a standard amount of living tissue. This leads to the *rad* unit, which is the dose that deposits 100 ergs of energy in 1 gramme of tissue. This is a very small amount of energy. For example, if it were heat, it would raise the temperature of the tissue by only 2 millionths of a degree. As high-energy radiation, however, this dose of energy ionises about one atom in 50,000 million. How much radiation would be needed to produce these effects? This important question concerns the link between the *curie* and *rad* units, which should relate radioactivity to its biological effects. However, a simple answer is not possible because the effects of exposure to a radioactive source vary greatly with circumstances, as we shall see in Chapter 5. As a specific example, if 1 cc of tissue were irradiated with 1 MeV electrons delivered from 0.0016 curies of a beta-emitting substance finely dispersed throughout this tissue, the dose would be about 1 rad per second.

The rad measures a radiation dose in terms of its *physical* effect, i.e. the amount of energy deposited. But when we come to *biological* effects a modified unit, the *rem*, is more useful. This is because some kinds of radiation are more powerful in their biological effects than others, and the rad unit needs to be corrected for this, by multiplying it with the *quality factor* of the radiation in question. What matters here is the nature of the trail of ionisations left along the track of the radiation particle or pulse. The same number of ionisations spread out thinly over a *long* track generally has less biological effect than when they are bunched together *thickly* within a *short* dense track. In other words, a given amount of ionisation generally causes more biological damage if it is all concentrated in a few cells rather than distributed sparsely over a large number. This effect distinguishes wave and electron radiations from the heavier nuclear particles. A gamma ray or

X-ray pulse, being highly penetrating through matter, leaves a long track consisting of widely-spaced small spots of ionisation. A high-energy electron (1 MeV) behaves similarly because, being a very light particle, it travels at high speed, and so there is little time for its electrical force to dislodge the electrons of each atom which it encounters along its track. By contrast an alpha particle, being much heavier, travels relatively slowly. It is also more strongly charged and so exerts greater electrical forces. As a result, it produces a short track of densely ionised atoms and for this reason is about 10 times as damaging as a gamma ray or beta particle. Hence, whereas 1 rad of gamma rays or beta particles also provides 1 rem of these radiations, in the case of alpha particles 1 rad provides about 10 rem. Generalising from this, the *rem* is that dose from any radiation which produces biological effects in mankind equivalent to 1 rad of X-rays.

Neutrons are electrically uncharged and so produce no ionisations themselves. Nevertheless, they are biologically damaging because they are deeply penetrating and release densely ionising particles from the nuclei of the tissue atoms which they encounter. There are two separate effects. A neutron may get absorbed into the nucleus of an atom of the host tissue and so make it radioactive—usually a gamma emitter. Or, if the neutron is a fast one, it may dislodge some of the nuclei it happens to meet in its path through the tissue and send these nuclei, crashing and ionising like alpha particles, into the nearby material. For these reasons the rem dose of neutrons, like that of alpha particles, is taken to be ten times the rad dose.

Hazardous doses

The main health effects of radiation fall into two distinct groups: the *short-term* effects of very heavy doses which appear soon afterwards and produce *radiation sickness* within days: and the *long-term* effects which can be produced by smaller doses and lead to various kinds of cancer, particularly leukaemia, and genetic effects which may appear many years later. Because the short-term effects occur characteristically in a matter of hours, radiation sickness is a result of heavy doses that are delivered *quickly*, i.e. also in at most a few hours. Heavy doses that are accumulated very gradually over long periods of time do not produce acute radiation sickness and their effects are of the long-term kind. As a result of this, our knowledge of radiation sickness, at least in its most severe forms, has come almost entirely from the victims of nuclear weapons, who have been exposed to massive amounts of radiation, large enough to damage cell membranes and to produce extensive internal bleeding, severe anaemia and seriously lowered resistance to infection. At Hiroshima those who received more than 1,000 rem of gamma radiation died within a week and most of those who received 700 rem died within two months. Other victims, such as the Japanese fishermen who were accidentally exposed to radiation from the testing of the first hydrogen bomb, and some American physicists who died from a nuclear accident in a weapons research laboratory, suffered in a similar way. The analysis of these cases has shown that a sudden whole-body dose of radiation greater than about 600 rem almost certainly leads to death within a matter of days or weeks. In the range around 300 rem about half of the victims, although made seriously ill with radiation sickness, have a chance of surviving. Doses below 200 rem produce no immediate effects although there will be long-term ill-health, particularly due to anaemia. Below 100 rem there are no obvious symptoms of radiation sickness, even though of course the long-term health hazards remain. Among the survivors of the Japanese atomic bombs were 24,000 who received about 130 rem each; they have since suffered over 100 cancer deaths more than is usual for a population of this size.

Large doses of radiation can be acquired gradually, a little at a time, with no radiation sickness. They may eventually make their effects felt in other ways, particularly by producing cancer after some years. Mankind has already experienced these long-term effects of large gradual doses, partly as a result of unfortunate early practices before the hazards of radiation were fully known, and partly as a result of calculated risks in the treatment of certain medical conditions with heavy doses of X-rays. These casualties include early scientists working on X-rays, as well as women employed early in the century to paint radium on luminous watch dials and underground miners exposed to the radioactive gas, *radon*, which occurs naturally in many localities. In addition, in Britain about 15,000 people were dosed with nearly 400 rem of X-rays each, for treatment of arthritis of the spine, and they suffered more than 100 excess cancer deaths. The treatment in Germany of almost 1,000 people with radium, also for arthritis of the spine, similarly led to about 50 excess cancer deaths. From the analysis of such information, the US *NAS-NRC Committee*[1] *on Biological Effects of Ionising Radiation* (BEIR) has estimated a likelihood of getting cancer from radiation which, in the range of doses experienced in the above cases, amounts to a one in fifty chance for someone exposed to 100 rem of whole-body radiation. By today's standards of radiological protection, 100 rem is a large dose, far above what the average person can expect to receive in a whole lifetime. The important question is: what is the likelihood of getting cancer from much smaller doses? We shall look at this in the next chapter.

Genetic defects are caused by molecular changes in the DNA in the chromosomes and genes of the reproductive cells. They occur naturally, as a result of spontaneous gene mutations, in about three percent of all live births, and produce various effects from colour blindness to major deformities. While experiments on insects and animals have suggested that high doses of radiation are able to produce genetic defects, there is little evidence in mankind. For example, there has been no more than the normal proportion of genetic defects in children born to the survivors of the Japanese atomic bombs. By contrast with this *genetic insensitivity* is the case of mothers who, in the days before radiation effects were fully appreciated, had been given high doses of abdominal radiation for medical purposes during pregnancy, amounting to hundreds of rem. These mothers generally produced severely deformed children, thereby demonstrating the sensitivity of the *foetus* to radiation.

The BEIR and other estimates suggest that if one million people each received 1 rem of radiation over 30 years, then there would be one or two significant genetic abnormalities per year produced by it in their children and about 10 a year in their ultimate descendants. By comparison, about 700 such abnormalities a year are produced by natural causes in a population of one million, i.e. about one in 17 births (assuming a birth rate of 1.2 per hundred). At such levels the genetic effect of radiation is thus very small compared with natural genetic changes; it does not become appreciable until doses of the order of 100 rem are reached.

Some efforts have been made to estimate the accumulated dose that would cause the rate of gene mutation to *double* its natural value. The *United Nations Scientific Committee on the Effects of Atomic Radiation* (UNSCEAR) concluded in 1962 that an accurate estimate is not possible, but their range of figures suggests that 30 rem is about the mutational doubling dose. For various biological reasons this doubling of the mutation rate is likely to produce less than a doubling of genetic defects. There is one set of mass observations which roughly bears out the figure. In a district of Kerala in India, inhabited by about 70,000 people, the thorium content of the soil provides a natural radiation dose in the range of 1.5 to 3.0 rem a year. Over the 30 year period during which most people have children a total dose in the range of 50 to 100 rcm is thus accumulated. Studies[2] of a large sample of this population have shown that, while no mutational effects on fertility, sex rates or infant mortality are evident, there is nevertheless an abnormally high occurrence of genetically-based mental retardation in children born to parents in this region. This rate is in fact some four times greater than that in a similar population chosen for comparison from a region free from such radiation. Radiation in the range 50 to 100 rem thus appears to quadruple the natural mutagenic rate for the development of this particular medical condition.

References

1   NAS-NRC refers to the National Academy of Sciences and the National Research Council who worked jointly on BEIR.
2   N. Kochupillai *et al*, *Nature*, 262, 60 (1976).

4

Is there a safe level of radiation?

The problem of low doses

If you had to give an opinion on the effects of low doses, but had only the results at high doses to guide you, what would you say? Would you take the high dose results and simply scale them down in direct proportion to the dose? This scaling down in simple proportion is in fact just what is done in practice, and is the basis of protective legislation for both radiation workers and the general public. An over-riding requirement in all civil nuclear energy work is that no-one should be exposed to doses even remotely approaching those at which the effects described in the last chapter begin to become a significant risk to health. The basic philosophy for all radiation work has been expressed by the International Commission on Radiological Protection (ICRP) in the principle of ALARA, i.e. to keep exposures 'as low as is reasonably achievable'. For all ordinary civil nuclear work we are thus concerned only with *low doses*, which are of necessity down in the range where their effects on health become imperceptible.

This leads straight to the question raised at the beginning of the paragraph above. How are we to make rules about effects which cannot be detected? Our only reliable evidence comes from those much larger doses, of the order of 100 rem, at which the biological and health effects can be measured and linked clearly to dose. All we can do about the low doses, where the effects shrink down into the general background of natural effects and chance variations, is to make indirect deductions by scaling down from high doses.

What method should be used for this scaling? The simplest is the *linear hypothesis*, which assumes that each effect is *simply proportional* to its dose, all the way down to zero dose. On this hypothesis there is no such thing as a safe dose, since even a near-zero exposure produces a *near-zero* effect, not a zero one. For example, if a 100 rem dose produces a 1 in 50 chance of cancer in the recipient, then a 1 rem dose gives a 1 in 5,000 chance and a 0.001 rem dose gives a 1 in 5 million chance. Such small individual chances are hard to grasp and impossible to recognise in practice. Because of this, they are best thought of as applying statistically to a large population. For example, if 5,000 people receive 1 rem each, then the linear hypothesis implies that one of them is likely to suffer cancer as a result. This leads to the idea of the *man-rem*: for example, 5,000 man-rem are expected to produce a single case of cancer irrespective of whether they are applied as 50 rem each to 100 people, or as 1 rem each to 5,000, or as 0.005 rem each to 1 million.

The linear hypothesis is widely accepted today as the basis of standards set for limiting the exposures of people to radiation. But it is only a hypothesis, not a proven law. How valid is it? As we scale the dose down, from high to low, could the effect scale down less sharply than the dose, or more so? Over the whole range to zero it could not scale down *less* sharply, for the simple reason that when the dose comes exactly to zero then so must its effect also. There are biological reasons in fact for believing that, as the dose is reduced, its effect should diminish *more* sharply and thereby reach zero at some small but non-zero dose. We have already noted that the same amount of ionisation is less damaging when spread out, in both space and time, than when highly concentrated. On this basis, the above example of 5,000 man-rem should lead to fewer cancers when applied as 1 rem to each of 5,000 people than as 50 rem to each of 100. There is also evidence from experiments on animals that doses of below 3 rem per week produce no detectable shortening of life, and that the time for radiation-induced cancer to appear is sufficiently long for smaller doses that, below a certain range of dose, it may exceed the natural lifetime of the creatures.

Such evidence, if it could be firmly established for mankind, would be particularly important for fixing a *safe* dose (or dose rate) below which radiation was not a risk to health. The scientific position is not really clear enough, however, to be able to say with confidence that there is a threshold below which doses are not damaging. The above argument about the concentration effect is a strong one. Against it, however, is the argument that the DNA molecule is the key target in the cell, as regards both health and genetics, and that a single 'hit' on this target can in principle seriously damage its structure. Against this, there is good laboratory evidence that most cells require several 'hits' before they are functionally damaged. And against that is the argument that a densely ionising particle, such as an alpha particle or an atom knocked aside by a neutron, can create so much concentrated havoc within a single cell as to be certain of producing many 'hits' in it.

Natural radiations

Overshadowing all these arguments, however, is the fact that all life on this planet has been continuously exposed to natural radiations for the whole of its 3,500 million years of evolution, from the most primitive cells to mankind, and that in every moment of our own lives we are all bathed in these radiations. On average each one of us receives from them an annual dose of about 0.1 rem (in other words a total of 3 rem per reproductive generation of 30 years), although the exact amount varies considerably from individual to individual according to location and mode of living. Almost one-half of the effect comes from *cosmic rays*, high energy radiations which the earth receives from outer space. Our atmosphere protects us from much of their direct action and also transforms them into various kinds of secondary radiations, such as gamma rays, high-speed electrons and other elementary particles such as mesons. The intensity of cosmic radiation approximately doubles in each 5,000 ft elevation above sea level, so that inhabitants of high alti- tude places such as Mexico City (7,350 ft) get over twice the normal dose. High flying jet aircraft also experience more intensive cosmic radiation and the crews of regularly operating airliners receive about 0.5 rem annually.

The other source of natural radiation is the earth itself, which contains various radioactive isotopes. The most important of these are *radon*−222, *radium*−226, some nuclear products of *thorium, potas- sium*−40, *carbon*−14 and *hydrogen*−3 (i.e. *tritium*). We experience the effects of some of these from soil, rocks and building materials. Some get taken into our bodies by breathing (e.g. radon), drinking and eating. For example, drinking waters vary by 10,000 times in their content of natural radioactive substances. Amongst foodstuffs, nuts and cereals contain larger amounts of radium than others. Finally, some substances exist naturally within our own bodies. Thus, potas- sium−40 and hydrogen−3 are important because potassium and hydrogen are essential constituents of living tissue. The annual personal dose of radiation from all these isotopes varies greatly with location and habit. We have already noted, at the end of the last chapter, the exceptionally high levels of up to 3 rem in Kerala, India, due to thorium in the local sands. Similar deposits along the coast of Brazil, near Rio de Janeiro, give an annual dose of up to 1 rem. Granite rocks are a common source of natural radioactivity. Thus the annual dose in, for example, Aberdeen (granite) is about 0.04 rem higher than that in London (sedimentary). Even within New York city the radiation level is 0.01 rem higher in Manhattan (granite) than in Brooklyn (sand). This is also significant in house construction for, although a house provides a shield against some external radiations, its materials contain naturally radioactive substances. A brick or stone house provides annually about 0.03 rem more than a wooden one; and a granite house can provide as much as 0.15 rem.

The amounts of natural radioactivity we receive can thus vary considerably, according to where and how we live. Yet, with the excep- tion of the genetic defect found in some children in Kerala, born to mothers who have received up to 100 rem over 30 years or so, there is no evidence that these wide variations have any effect whatsoever on health. People normally do not give the slightest thought to such possi- bilities when choosing, for example, whether to live in Aberdeen, New

Mexico or London; and they are right not to do so, for there is no evidence for any biologically or medically significant differences between these radioactively different places. Does this mean that annual doses less than about 0.5 rem, i.e. less than 15 rem in 30 years, fall below a safe threshold? We do not know, simply because there are no detectable effects in this range. It may be that the genetic molecule, DNA, is able to repair radiation damage produced at such low rates. Life has, after all, evolved in an environment of radiation and living cells are known to have remarkably high abilities to repair their DNA. Most DNA is reproduced, from generation to generation, with extraordinary precision despite all the mutagenic hazards (such as various chemicals) to which it is exposed. Yet, a few genetic changes do occur and are passed on. For the progress of evolution some genetic change is essential; and a population of a given species could survive the loss of a small number of radiation victims, provided that the majority are enabled to evolve satisfactorily. Thus evolution may have developed only a high tolerance of low-level radiation, not a complete resistance to it.

It follows that we have no clear answer to the question of whether a threshold exists below which radiation is completely safe. Consistent with this, *no such threshold is assumed* in the regulatory standards for exposure to radiation. These are based on the *linear hypothesis*, even though this is thought by many students of the subject to be overcautious at low doses.

Dose limits

The assumption that the effects of radiation continue in direct proportion to the dose, all the way down to zero dose, means that the setting of permissible dose limits has to be done by an act of *judgement*, a balancing of risks due to low-dose radiations against benefits from the activities leading to them, whether medical or economic. In addition to general rationality and good sense, the two qualities required to make sound judgements are *independence* and *expert knowledge*. Rightly, these are provided by the International Commission on Radiological Protection (ICRP), which is the body that makes generally accepted recommendations for limits to radiation doses. In existence since the 1920s, it is independent of governments and the United Nations, and consists at present of twelve scientists from various countries. They are chosen purely on the basis of their professional standing, independently of approval by governments, by the International Congress of Radiology, an entirely professional body.

When drawing up dose limits it is necessary to consider separately three different classes of people: workers in occupations which involve radiation; patients receiving radiation for medical benefits; and the general public. Many individuals these days receive radiation through their work; for example in medicine and dentistry, nuclear power, industrial radiography, scientific research, some mines and in high-flying aircraft. The main hazard for them is cancer. Because they are adult (and so lack the extra vulnerability of young children), are generally in good health and subjected to medical examination, and are a small part of the total population, they are generally permitted a higher dose limit than the general public. The ICRP recommended limit is 5 rems a year for whole-body radiation (apart from natural and medical contributions). In addition, other limits are also often set: e.g. no exposure to such radiation below the age of 18; accumulated life-time dose not to exceed a certain amount, e.g. 25 rem. The 5 rem rate is about 50 times the average natural radiation rate, and in practice radiation workers are often exposed to rates of 10 times the natural average. The above dose limits in fact correspond to a rate somewhat higher than, and a total dose somewhat lower than, those experienced from natural radiation in Kerala, which produces a small incidence of genetic abnormality in children of exposed mothers, but seemingly no other effects. In practical terms, therefore, these limits appear to be about at the point where the clinical symptoms of radiation first begin to become statistically detectable in a large population.

The problem of miners exposed to radon gas is a special case. In the past, before the harmful effects of large exposures were fully realized, some miners breathed in large doses; and a proportion of them, well above the national average, died of lung cancer. While the exact causes of these lung cancers are hard to trace, limits have now been set on permissible amounts of radon that can be inhaled at work; and mines are now ventilated to provide a safe atmospheric environment.

Radiation for *medical purposes* is widely used these days. In Britain the total annual dose averages about 0.03 rem, although there are of course enormous variations between individuals. In other countries (e.g. USA, Japan, Sweden) the totals run higher and are about the same as natural radiation (i.e. about 0.1 rem a year). In the case of certain serious illnesses, very large amounts of radiation may be applied locally to particular parts of the body for therapeutic reasons —sufficiently so in extreme cases to pose a real radiation hazard to the individual in question. Here it is a straight balance of benefit versus risk, on the basis of an informed medical judgement. Where the benefit is clearly greater than the risk, then the treatment will be recommended. Because of this, the main general concern about the large-scale use of medical radiation is the *genetic* risk to the general population, although heavy medical radiations are today rarely used except for the treatment of cancers.

For individual members of the *general public*—which includes of course all age groups, from infants to the aged and infirm, as well as expectant mothers and ill people—the ICRP recommendation is that the limiting dose should be one-tenth of that of radiation workers, i.e. 0.5 rem a year; and that for entire populations, where the genetic risk becomes important, it should be only one-thirtieth of the radiation workers' dose. These recommendations have been largely accepted, sometimes with additional provisos, by governments. For example, the British government's policy was set down in a 1959 White Paper on 'The Control of Radioactive Wastes' (Command 884) as follows:

1 To ensure, irrespective of cost, that no member of the public shall be exposed to a radiation dose exceeding the ICRP limit.

2 To ensure, irrespective of cost, that the whole population of the country shall not receive an average dose of more than 1 rem per person in 30 years.

3 To do what is reasonably practical, having regard to cost, to reduce doses to far below these levels.

It will be noticed that the ICRP limit is *below* the natural level in regions of high radiation in Kerala and Brazil; and that the limit in 2 above is below the ordinary natural level (0.1 rem a year). The third of the above requirements is fully satisfied by the nuclear power industry at present, which contributes almost negligibly to the radiation dose experienced by the general public. The following table shows the 1978 figures for Britain:

Annual radiation experienced by the general public

| Source | Rem per person, average | |
	1978	30 year total
Natural	0.096	2.9
Medical radiation	0.030	0.9
Fallout from weapons tests	0.002	0.06
Occupational	0.0007	0.02
Air travel	0.0006	0.02
Luminous watches	0.0002	0.006
Nuclear wastes	0.0002	0.006

We see that, while the average level of medical radiation comes close to the limit 2 above, although well below the natural level, the problem of the level from nuclear wastes is an unreal one at the present time and belongs to the realm of imagined future possibilities.

Some dissenting views

The difficulties of estimating the effects of radiation at low doses, where these merge into the general background of other effects and where the linear hypothesis has to be used to obtain any real guidance at all, are such that no-one would wish to defend the values to within a factor of two or three. They are round figures, not precise values. Thus we are led to expect, in round terms, that each rem of whole-body radiation provides an additional 1 in 10,000 chance of its recipient dying from cancer; and that an accumulated dose of 30 rem, e.g. 1 rem for each of the 30 years of a reproductive generation, may produce a rate of genetic mutation of double its natural value.

What matters is not the exact value of these figures, but their general order of magnitude. Could they be wrong by, say, a factor of 10? If, as some people believe, there is a threshold, then the actual effects at low doses may be very much less than these figures suggest. The penalty for this error is an economic one, through the expense of unnecessarily stringent safety restrictions. But, as regards public safety, the question of greatest interest is the other possibility. Could the health effects of radiation at low doses be 10 or more times greater than are suggested by these figures? Several critics of the orthodox radiation estimates have argued this.

Everyone—the orthodox and their critics—have of course to start from the same point, i.e. to work from the same published 'raw' data on the various effects. The arguments thus arise, not over the data as such, but over the methods by which these are analysed and interpreted. And because the data at low doses are concerned with necessarily weak effects, the number of positive examples of such effects in a given sample is always rather small. This opens the way to all kinds of errors and controversy, because small numbers are prone to large random variations, which may be misread as significant trends, and because it is extremely difficult to disentangle significant weak effects from false indications due to various stray extraneous influences.

For example, out of a million people approximately 200,000 inevitably die from cancer. If this million were to receive 1 rem each of radiation, their cancer deaths would be expected to rise to 200,100, an increase which is far smaller than the normal variations to be expected in such a statistical quantity as the basic 200,000. But, even if the orthodox calculations had underestimated the cancer rate from radiation by a factor of 10, the increase would still be only to 201,000 i.e. by half-a-percent, which is in the range of normal statistical fluctuations and so could not be recognised with certainty in practice. The cancer rate from radiation would have to be 100 times above the orthodox value for its effect to become noticeable at the 1 rem per person level. However, even if it were only 10 times the orthodox value it would still have shown up devastatingly among the Japanese atomic bomb victims. We recall that 24,000 survivors received about 130 rem each and that rather over 100 of them died later from cancer attributed to this radiation. But if the cancer rate had been 1 in 1000 per rem, then over 3,000 would have died, a figure which undoubtedly would have resounded throughout all modern analyses of radiation hazards, since it would then have been nearly equal to the natural cancer death rate.

To take another example, the accumulated natural radiation received by 30 year old mothers in Kerala is about 50 to 100 rems. If the orthodox value underestimates the genetic damage by a factor of 10, then the mutational doubling dose should be only about 3 rems and the proportion of genetically retarded children born to these mothers should be some 30 times the general average, instead of the observed value of about 4 times. There would also be noticeable effects among children born to long service airline stewardesses. To take a non-genetic example, during its nine months in the womb an infant in Britain receives some 0.075 rem of natural radiation. If, as some critics have suggested, the infantile leukaemia rate were as high as three in 1,000 per rem, then more than 200 children per million should suffer from leukaemia due to this cause alone. But 200 per million is the total figure, for children in Britain, due to *all* causes of leukaemia.

We see that the risks to health of low radiation doses cannot, even at worst, be much larger than are estimated by the orthodox calculations, since otherwise they would have already revealed themselves in various spectacular ways.

5

Which radioactive substances are dangerous?

The important physical factors

Over 100 different kinds of isotopes are created in a nuclear reactor. Many of them are radioactive. Which are the main hazards to health? The answer depends on many different things. The most obvious factors to start with are the amounts of each substance that are produced in the reactor, their half-lives, and their types of radioactivity.

Broadly, radioactive substances in nuclear reactors fall into three main groups, according to how they are produced. First are the *fission products*, the new atoms formed out of the split fragments of uranium nuclei. Mostly, these are a large group of various isotopes, all with nuclei in the 'middle' range of sizes, half of them having about 85 to 105 particles (protons and neutrons); and the other half having about 130 to 150. Generally, they are beta and gamma emitters. Many have short half-lives, of no more than a few minutes or hours, and very few have half-lives longer than a year.

Next are the substances with heavy nuclei, the *actinides*, which are formed from uranium nuclei by the capture, without fission, of one or more neutrons. The most important of these is *plutonium*–239, but there are several other plutonium isotopes, as well as several isotopic variants of other actinides such as *americium* and *curium*. The actinides are mostly alpha emitters and have long half-lives. That of plutonium–239 for example is 24,000 years.

The third group is less close-knit because it consists of all those substances produced by various secondary processes. One of the main examples is *hydrogen*–3 (tritium), a beta emitter with a half-life of 12 years, which is produced by an unusual kind of fission in which the uranium nucleus splits into *three* parts, one of which is the tritium nucleus. It is also produced by neutron reactions with boron and hydrogen–2 nuclei. Neutrons are directly responsible for several important substances in this third group, notably *carbon*–14, which is a beta emitter (5,800 years) produced by the action of neutrons on certain nitrogen and oxygen nuclei. This long half-life has made naturally produced carbon−14 a useful substance for archaeological dating. Neutrons can combine with many nuclei to form radioisotopes, and for this reason it is important to use very pure materials inside reactors, so as to avoid impurities that could wastefully absorb neutrons and at the same time become radioactive nuisances.

To these three categories we should add a fourth, those *natural* radioactive substances released by the mining of uranium ore, and the conversion of this ore into nuclear fuel for the reactor. The most important substances of this kind are *radon* and *radium*, both alpha emitters.

Many radioisotopes produced in reactors have very short half-lives and virtually disappear within a few seconds, minutes or hours of their formation. The *delayed neutrons* which are important for the stable running of reactors are one product of some of these short-lived nuclei. For example, the commonly produced *bromine*−87 nucleus decays in about 1 minute to the stable isotope of *krypton*, with the emission of a neutron. *Iodine*−137 decays with a 23 second half-life by a similar process. These very short-lived isotopes are of little significance for public safety because they decay inside the reactor, almost as soon as they are formed. Even in a quick release due to a sudden reactor accident they would largely have vanished before reaching the general public.

Several radioisotopes have half-lives in the range of days or weeks. For example, that of *iodine*−131, an important fission product, is eight days. The practice of transferring nuclear fuel elements to deep water cooling ponds for about six months, immediately they are removed from their reactor, ensures that the radioactivity due to such isotopes as these has largely decayed before the fuel elements are exposed for reprocessing. For example, six months 'cooling' reduces the activity of iodine−131 to less than a millionth of its initial value.

Finally, there is the group of more long-lived radioisotopes, which persist for months and years. These include beta-emitting fission products such as *ruthenium*−106, with a one year half-life, *strontium*−90, with a 28 year half-life, and *caesium*−137, with a 30 year half-life, which are troublesome when reprocessing irradiated fuel elements after removal from the ponds; and also the actinides such as *plutonium* and other substances such as *carbon*−14.

Next to the nuclear characteristics is the importance of the physical state of existence of a radioactive substance. As regards their general chemical and physical properties, radioisotopes are just like the ordinary forms of the substances in question; and so we are concerned at this stage with ordinary physico-chemical behaviour. Many radioactive substances, for example strontium−90 and ruthenium−106, remain ordinarily in solid form at ordinary temperatures (and so cannot spread far unless there is a major accident, involving release to the atmosphere at high temperatures), or they are converted into soluble compounds and dissolved in, for example, water. But some exist naturally as gases and have a particular importance for this reason. These include *krypton*−85 and *xenon*−133, beta emitters with half-lives of 11 years and 5 days, respectively; and *argon*−41, a beta and gamma emitter with a 2 hour half-life, as well as iodine and tritium. Mostly, the gaseous fission products remain locked up inside the nuclear fuel itself, or in the metal cans which are sealed round the fuel. But inevitably small amounts sometimes escape through occasional defects in the cans. The main release, however, comes later, when the irradiated fuel is removed from the cooling pond and stripped down for reprocessing. This is important in the case of krypton−85, for this, because of its long half-life, is practically all released into the air during reprocessing. Most of the tritium also escapes into the air, whereas the short-lived xenon and iodine are much less important under ordinary reactor-operating and fuel-reprocessing conditions.

The important biological factors

The physical properties of the radioactive substances are only half of the story. The biological properties ultimately determine the extent to which a substance of given radioactivity is a health hazard. What matters here is the tendency of a substance to find its way to the body, into critical organs inside the body, and then to stay there in high local concentration; it is this tendency that makes some radioisotopes particularly dangerous. In their biological properties, the radioisotopes behave just like ordinary atoms of the substance, and so their various 'pathways' to, in and through the body are determined by standard biochemical processes. A radioactive change is a single, sudden, event in the life of an unstable nucleus, which for all the rest of its time behaves exactly the same as a stable nucleus and gives no sign of its radioactivity.

Radioactive substances may get taken into the body through breathing, eating or drinking, and they may also enter through cuts in the skin. Not surprisingly, many different pathways to the body are followed by particular substances. Gases of course enter through the lungs. Small solid particles which float as dust in the air may also be breathed in, but they tend then to stay in the lungs. Tritium may become chemically combined as water and so get breathed in as vapour or drunk as liquid; carbon−14 may likewise be taken up in carbon dioxide, another basic constituent of ordinary air and mineral waters; and both tritium and carbon−14 may enter, as basic hydrogen and carbon constituents of biological substances, any part of the living world including our own bodies.

Some substances get into foodstuffs. Strontium behaves chemically like calcium and so finds its way into all those places in living organisms where calcium goes. Caesium similarly behaves like potassium, another biochemically important element. Caesium−137 is important because, when discharged into the sea in dilute, low-activity waste, it is selectively absorbed by fish and shellfish. Measured on a national scale the amounts are small, but a few fishermen who live off catches taken from the Irish sea near the Windscale reprocessing plant absorb about 0.2 rem a year in this way.

An important isotope in the case of sudden accidental releases is *iodine*–131, because it can find its way into milk and thence into the thyroid gland. In 1957 an accident occurred at Windscale to an early type of reactor, which was open to the air. Several tons of uranium melted and released their more volatile contents to the atmosphere through a chimney stack. In this way about 20,000 curies of radio-iodine escaped and spread, downwind, on about 200 square miles of grassland used by dairy herds. About 5 percent of the iodine eaten, in grass, finds its way into cow's milk and because of this all milk supplies from the affected region were stopped for a time long enough to allow the activity from the iodine–131 (half life = 8 days) to decay.

This radio-iodine is a dangerous substance because, in the body, it concentrates in the thyroid gland where it can produce cancer. However, the risk of this can be reduced if, immediately after a release, the people in the affected region take pills containing a digestible compound of ordinary iodine. In this way, their glands can be temporarily satiated with ordinary iodine, so that they will then not accept the radio-iodine.

Just as the thyroid gland is the critical organ for radio-iodine, and the lungs for airborne particles, so various other parts of the body are vulnerable to particular radioactive substances. Soluble substances tend to collect in the kidneys and reproductive organs. Krypton, breathed into the lungs, goes into body fat. The bones are particularly vulnerable and collect plutonium, strontium and other substances where the local radiation may produce tumours, as well as irradiating the important bone marrow. Plutonium and strontium are particularly dangerous because they stay in the bones and irradiate them for many years. By contrast, some radioisotopes are rapidly eliminated from the body and so their effect is less than might otherwise be expected. For example, half of a tritium intake is eliminated from the body in about 8 days and thus, despite its radioactive half life of 12 years, its *effective* half-life—so far as its potency as a health hazard is concerned—is only 8 days. Even plutonium is fairly harmless if swallowed (instead of being inhaled) because it is then quickly excreted.

Maximum permissible burdens

The detailed knowledge that has gradually been built up, about where radioactive substances go and the effects they have on critical organs, has enabled the general ICRP recommended dose limits to be developed into a list of maximum permissible amounts of various particular substances that can be taken into the body. In the case of *plutonium*–239 in bone, for example, the *maximum permissible body burden*

(MPBB) is 0.04 microcuries (1 microcurie = 1 millionth of a curie). How was this figure obtained? The story goes back to the experience of the early workers with radium for this is, like plutonium, a bone-seeking alpha-emitting substance. Many of these workers collected from one to upwards of 10 microcuries of radium in their bodies; and as a result some developed bone tumours. From detailed comparisons of the amounts taken in and the development of bone cancer, many years later, a limit was then set of not more than 0.1 microcuries of radium to be present in the body of a radium worker. When plutonium was discovered and the need for a MPBB value recognised, the radium experience provided the starting point. However, because radium spreads throughout bone material, whereas plutonium remains on the surface of bone, and because plutonium is rather more toxic than radium, an additional restriction was placed on the limit. The MPBB for plutonium was thus set at 0.04 microcuries. Since, because of its long half-life (24,000 years for plutonium, 1,600 years for radium), plutonium has only one-fifteenth the radioactivity of the same weight of radium, this MPBB amounts to a limit in bone of 0.6 micrograms of plutonium.

Corresponding maximum permissible burdens in the whole body, and in critical organs, have been deduced for other radioactive substances, and are recommended by the ICRP as secondary standards which fall within their basic rem dose standards. As with the latter, the limits set for the general public are one-tenth of those for radiation workers.

Consistent with this, *maximum permissible concentrations* (MPC) of various radioactive substances have been set, which correspond to the recommended ICRP rem dose limits. These MPC values have been derived by monitoring the environmental conditions to which radiation workers are exposed during a standard working week, and then relating the environmental radiation to the maximum dose that such a worker would then experience. For example, in drinking water the MPCs of tritium, strontium−90, and radium−226, in microcuries per litre, are 200, 0.004 and 0.0004 respectively. Similarly, the MPC of radon gas in air is 0.00001 microcurie per litre. The setting of trustworthy MPC values is difficult, because it depends on the identification and analysis of all the various possible pathways by which different radioactive substances can find their ways into the bodies of radiation workers and members of the general public; and also upon estimation of the likely amounts to be taken in under various circumstances. Fortunately, the policy of erring on the side of caution leads to a simplification of the analysis, because it enables the investigation to seek out and concentrate on *critical groups* of people; that is those people who, because of their personal circumstances, are exposed to distinctly higher doses than average. The fishermen eating their catches off the Cumbrian coast are an example. By setting limits at insignificant doses for these critical groups, there is assurance that the public generally is not hazarded by such pathways.

6

According to plan

Allowed releases of radioactivity

Sooner or later every radioactive atom created in a reactor has to be disposed of, by one way or another. In fact 99.9% of them transform of their own accord, either by nuclear reactions while they are still inside the reactor, or in the cooling ponds in which the fuel elements are quarantined after being in the reactor. Nevertheless, during the normal running of a reactor small amounts of radioactive substances do escape into the general surroundings; and more are released, dilutely, as low-activity gases or in waste water from the ponds and the fuel reprocessing plant. How large are these allowed releases? How do they compare with the ICRP recommended limits? How much of a hazard are they to us?

Before we look into these questions, it is useful to remember how enormous the oceans and atmosphere are, as repositories of highly dispersed and sparsely distributed substances. For example, the oceans contain as a natural constituent about 4,000 million tons of uranium together with all its various radioactive products, including radium. But this vast store of radioactivity is spread through more than a million million million tons of water, so dilutely as to be economically hardly worthwhile considering as a source of fuel for thermal reactors. Again, in the atmosphere there are about 60 million curies of radioactive tritium, produced naturally by the actions of cosmic rays. But these are spread so extremely thinly throughout 5,000 million million tons of air as to be virtually undetectable—and certainly far below the levels at which any medical effects could make themselves felt.

The same dilution effect is important for the allowed releases of radioactive substances from nuclear reactors and reprocessing plants. Take for example krypton−85. A 1,000 megawatt (electrical) nuclear power station produces about 10 lbs a year. On the extreme assumption that all of this krypton−85 gets into the air and stays there for all of its 11-year radioactive half-life, then 1,000 such reactors would produce a steady content of about 50 tons in the atmosphere. Fully dispersed, this amounts to about 1 part in 100 million million, from which the dose rate is about 5 millionths of a microcurie per litre, which is over 500 times smaller than the ICRP's recommended maximum permissible occupational concentration.

Similarly for dilution in water. Consider as a hypothesis the River Thames as a medium for carrying away nuclear waste. About 3,000 million tons of water a year flow down it. At this rate it could in principle be given up to 1½ tons of plutonium a year, in soluble form, and yet still be drinkable, within the maximum permissible occupational concentration of plutonium. When considering dilute solutions of radioactive substances in water it is often useful to evaluate them in terms of their *toxic potential*. This is the amount of water in which a given quantity of the (soluble) substance would have to be dissolved, in order to reach that degree of dilution recommended by the ICRP for drinking water in continuous use. The River Thames estimate, above, corresponds to a toxic potential of 30 million litres per curie of plutonium. Clearly, from this purely hypothetical example, even a moderate natural body of water has the capacity to carry a substantial amount of a dangerous substance, in solution, in such great dilution as to be safely drinkable.

Releases from reactors

How much radioactivity is released from reactors during normal running? In Britain there are now records, going back many years, of the long-running, gas-cooled, graphite-moderated, *Magnox* reactors. The earliest types of these release argon−41 gas, from air used to cool the reactor shield, and measurements at the edge of the reactor site give a dose rate due to this gas of about 0.01 rem per year, i.e. one-tenth of the average natural radiation rate. The later types of Magnox reactors, which use water-cooled shielding—and also the somewhat similar AGR reactors—release much less argon−41 than this. Overall, the total release in Britain from all Magnox reactors amounts to little more than 100 man-rem a year. Very small amounts of iodine−131 and carbon−14 are also released, but samples of milk taken from farms near such reactors have no detectable content of iodine−131.

It would of course be both surprising and disturbing if the radioactivity released from a reactor, as a result of its normal running, were allowed to set any significant hazard—even if confined to those members of the general public who happened to live near the reactor site. In fact, measurements made by the United Nations Scientific Committee on the Effects of Atomic Radiation (UNSCEAR)[1] at the boundary fences of 24 nuclear power stations in seven different countries, gave doses in all cases well within the ICRP limit of 0.5 rem a year for the general public. The 22 more modern of these nuclear stations gave doses that were only about one-hundredth of the ICRP limit.

Some waste water is released from gas-cooled reactors and it contains tritium and caesium−137, as well as traces of other radioactive sub-stances. Mostly it is discharged in dilute form into the sea, locally, and this has been shown by regular surveys to have a negligible effect. The most extreme cases are where it is discharged into a lake, e.g. Lake Trawsfynydd which serves a nuclear power station in North Wales. There is an extreme possibility here for someone, regularly eating large catches of fish from such a lake, to receive about 0.015 rem a year from this source.

The annual discharge of waste water from all Magnox reactors provides a total dose of about 50 man-rem, mainly from caesium−137 in coastal waters. On average, the amounts of tritium released in reactor waste water are about 3 percent of the authorised limit and those of other radioactive substances are about 25 percent of the limit.

The position is much the same with water-cooled reactors. There can be a gaseous release of xenon; but with standard precautions, the maximum dose rate from this release at the boundary of the reactor site is held down to about the same as that of argon from gas-cooled reactors. The traces of iodine and krypton released into the atmosphere from such reactors are also insignificant; the same is true of tritium, in waste water. Even including the contributions of additional releases of krypton and tritium gases, during the treatment of spent fuel elements in the reprocessing plant, the total annual dose per person in the USA would be less than 0.00025 rem, were the entire output of electricity in USA to be supplied from water reactors. This is only about one five-hundredth of the annual dose from natural radiation. In fact, it has now become possible for the US regulatory authorities, by applying the ALARA principle to this favourable situation, to lower the whole-body limits for the general public to 0.025 rem a year. Even though these new limits are only one-twentieth of the ICRP recommendations, and also only one-fifth of the average natural dose (as well as being only one-sixth of the *difference* in natural doses experienced in various parts of the USA), nevertheless they still exceed the *actual* releases from normally operating reactors by a large margin.

Clearly, a nuclear power station, in its normal operations, poses no significant hazard to public health through its radioactive releases.

Releases from spent fuel

Most of a reactor's radioactive substances are both made and held inside the fuel elements. When spent fuel is taken from its reactor it usually contains, in addition to unused uranium, up to about 3 percent by weight of fission product atoms of various kinds, as well as about 1 percent of actinide elements, mostly plutonium. Since the shorter-lived elements disappear while the fuel elements are in the cooling ponds, only the longer-lived ones may get released during reprocessing. At the reprocessing plant the fuel elements are cut up, their cladding removed, and dissolved in nitric acid. This is then treated chemically to extract the uranium and plutonium separately, for further use. Finally the highly radioactive and concentrated solutions of fission product waste are stored in extremely secure tanks.

Some gaseous radioactive elements escape into the atmosphere during these processes. The most important is krypton−85, but there is also tritium in water vapour, as well as a little carbon−14 and iodine−129. Dilute waste water is also discharged from the plant. Its most important radioactive constituent is caesium−137, but there are others, including a little plutonium. The amounts that are allowed to be released are all controlled by the government's regulatory authorities at levels which are below, in some cases very much below, the ICRP limits.

The amounts released from reprocessing plants are more significant than those from reactors. The gaseous releases are not at present important—in Britain they give a total of about 200 man-rem a year—but they may become so if the amount of nuclear reprocessing increases greatly. The important constituent, krypton, can be removed by a freezing process applied to the outgoing gases, and plans are under consideration for incorporating this in future reprocessing plants. It would have the additional advantage of removing carbon−14 from the released gases. At present, carbon−14 does not pose a significant hazard, but it has an extremely long half-life, 5,800 years; and so the amount introduced into the environment by a continuing programme of nuclear power will not level off to some steady value, but will continue to increase steadily over many years. In the long term it could eventually reach high levels, if not removed.

Of more immediate importance is the waste water from reprocessing plants, which releases significant amounts of caesium−137, as well as traces of plutonium and other substances. At Windscale, for example, about 18 million curies of caesium−137 are processed each year, of which about 30,000 are released into the Irish Sea from a pipeline extending 2½ kilometres from the Cumbrian coast. Some of this gets into fish and shellfish which people eat. Local fishermen are most at risk and extreme cases have been reported in which the amounts eaten gave doses of 30 to 40 percent of the ICRP limit. However, new treatment systems planned at Windscale are expected to reduce these releases considerably.

The total release to Britain from all radioactive waste is estimated to be about 10,000 man-rem a year. It is of course a *very small* total dose compared with that which the British population receives from natural radiation (about 5 million man-rem a year) which possibly produces half to one percent of all cancer deaths in the country.

Releases from mining

Uranium is mined in various parts of the world. It is separated chemically, in the form of 'yellowcake' oxide, from its powdered ore and then shipped to the fuel-making plant (e.g. Springfields in Britain) where it is purified and made into fuel pellets. Uranium is radioactive but its half-life is so long (4,500 million years) that its activity is extremely low and it presents no significant radioactive hazard. However, in its natural and unpurified form it contains small amounts of its various radioactive products and, because of this, is a source of *radon* gas. Radon is an important hazard in underground mining—especially in uranium mines, but in others as well. It may be partly responsible for the prevalence of lung cancer among miners, although they can be protected from it (as well as from other harmful agents, such as dust) by proper ventilation of the mines.

The release of radon from a uranium mine and its associated mine dump is important locally because, over the site of the workings, it can amount to a few hundred times the world average *natural* releases of radon from sites of comparable size. This is slightly hazardous to people living nearby, but the releases could be substantially reduced by covering finished dumps with asphalt and earth.

Away from the mine itself, however, the dilution effect of the atmosphere renders this radon insignificant, compared with world-wide natural releases. Even if all the world's electricity were made from thermal nuclear reactors, and even if the old mine dumps were all left exposed to the air, the mining needed to supply one year of this power would add only one part in 6,000 to the natural radon content of the atmosphere.

A sense of proportion

How much radiation should be allowed to reach the general public? None? That would be impossible, of course, because of natural radiation. None other than natural, then? But that would bring in great penalties, for it would rule out medical treatment by radiation, as well as nuclear electricity. It would also be illogical to forbid this, while at the same time leaving people exposed to unnecessarily large amounts of natural radiation because they live near granite, or on hill-tops, or travel by air, or engage in mining or burn coal which releases radioactive impurities in its smoke and ash.

Clearly there has to be some commonsense about all this: a sense of proportion. Rational people do not take seriously the notion that they may be significantly at risk from radiation because they live in Aberdeen rather than London (or Manhattan rather than Brooklyn). If assurance is nevertheless needed on this point, the official mortality figures (deaths per 100,000 in the year 1976) showed Aberdeen as slightly better placed than London for both leukaemia (6.7 as against 7) and other forms of cancer (253 as against 263); but commonsense tells us that such slight numerical differences as these are merely statistical fluctuations, devoid of significance.

Should then the exposure of the general public to man-made

radiation be limited to something above zero but smaller than the average natural dose? For example, to not more than 0.025 rem a year? This small figure would in fact exclude a lot of medical radiation and could thus be justifiably opposed on health grounds. But the figure would quite easily let in nuclear power, on the basis of *actual* releases from standard operations which give doses of generally less than 1 percent of the average natural amount. Not surprisingly, in view of the smallness of the nuclear doses, as compared with even the *geographical variations* of the natural ones, there has been no significant detectable effect on public health due to living near or far from nuclear installations. For example, the mortality figures (on the same basis as those given above) for Cumbria were 6.5 deaths due to leukaemia (national average = 6.3) and 252 due to all cancers (national average = 246). As regards atomic energy workers themselves, whether still active or retired and pensioned, the death rate from all cancers including leukaemia (measured in 1972) was 85 per cent of that expected from national rates for these diseases. The same commonsense that makes radiation a negligible consideration when deciding whether to live in Aberdeen or London should apply equally when deciding whether to live near or far from Windscale.

Reference

1   Reported by W. G. Marley, *Atomic energy and the environment*, National Radiological Protection Board, Report NRPB-R6, December 1972.

7

When things go wrong

Alarm at Harrisburg

As we have seen, nuclear reactors are rather harmless power producers so long as things go right. But what if things go wrong? The arguments of the last chapter would have given little comfort to the inhabitants of Harrisburg and other communities living near the Three Mile Island reactor, in Pennsylvania, on 28 March 1979. Just after 4.00 a.m. that morning the pumps which feed water to the boilers cut out. This was a routine and easily correctible fault, but at Three Mile Island it set off a chain of consequences, including some critical mistakes by the operators and at least one malfunction by an important reactor valve, which escalated the incident rapidly into what became the most alarming accident in the history of civil nuclear power.

Over the next few days the civic authorities and general public living in the nearby communities became intensely alarmed. Yet the major safety systems of the reactor all came into action automatically as soon as they were signalled to do so, and the radioactivity was almost entirely contained within the reactor building. From the small amounts that did escape, no-one received as much as one year's dose of natural radioactivity, and the average received within 5 miles of the reactor was only as much as one month's natural dose. The public was not physically harmed by Three Mile Island. But the local inhabitants suffered enormous nervous strain.

Basically, of course, this was for a very formidable reason— the great potential danger to health from the 10,000 million or so curies of radioactivity in the stricken reactor. However, there were various kinds of barriers and safety features to prevent that radioactivity getting out of the reactor, and they very largely succeeded in this. Why then was there such lack of faith in these protective devices? Partly it was because, although the fission reaction itself had been completely shut down right from the start of the accident, the operators were not able to get the reactor fully under control until some days later. It was during this time that the well-known bubble of hydrogen gas formed, and appeared to threaten a major hydrogen-oxygen explosion inside the reactor—although this was later proved to be not possible.

But the public's fears were unnecessarily exacerbated, because they were badly served in what they were, or rather were not, told about nuclear safety. They were particularly badly served by the nuclear authorities themselves, who failed to set out the facts fully, openly and promptly during the critical early stages, thereby undermining public confidence in official statements. The public had also been badly prepared by undue official secrecy beforehand, and by the activities of anti-nuclear campaigners who had fed them with vivid articles, films and TV programmes of a deliberately alarmist kind. And during the incident itself some (but not all) news reporters and commentators unwarrantably sensationalised the incident with stories so lurid ('a nuclear cloud is floating towards east coast cities') that badly-informed people were driven into a state of terror.

From the alarming to the absurd

This playing on public nerves did not start and finish at Harrisburg. It has applied also—and far less justifiably—to all kinds of lesser incidents in nuclear plants, such as small leaks, all the way down to minor occurrences of the kind that happen commonly in even the best run of industries. These have often been misrepresented to the general public under dramatic and scarifying headlines. Not surprisingly, the real and important issues of nuclear safety have in this way frequently been obscured by swarms of over-inflated petty happenings; and civic representatives of the public interest have thereby been led to call for precautionary measures not altogether unlike those of Alice's White Knight (in *Through the Looking Glass*) who, it will be remembered, fixed anklets round his horse's feet to ward off sharks, presumably in central Oxfordshire.

Take for example the recent call by some London borough councils to forbid the transport of nuclear waste by rail through the city. After nuclear fuel has been removed from a reactor and stored in the cooling ponds, which eliminates 90 percent of its radioactivity, it is (in Britain) taken to Windscale by rail in 50 ton thick steel containers. Each of these holds up to 200 fuel rods, in about 200 gallons of water, and each fuel rod generates a few watts of heat from its remaining 1,600 curies of activity. The containers are designed and constructed to standards set by the International Atomic Energy Agency and have also to be approved by British Rail and the government's Department of Transport. The intention is that a container should remain fully intact under every kind of accident, whether a collision, a fire or a mere overturning due, for example, to a derailment. For this purpose, various tests are applied. For example, quarter-scale models are dropped from 30 ft on to a solid, hard, steel and concrete base from various angles, and required to remain unbreached. Similarly, full-sized containers are exposed to a half-hour petrochemical fire on all sides at a temperature not below 800°C.

In practice, a container is carried on a large transporter, which would absorb much of the blow during a collision, and thereby soften the impact. The temperatures of conventional fires are too low to melt the fuel, so that, during a conflagration, most of the radioactive product would be expected to remain locked-up inside the solid material. The chance of a breach of a container is thus virtually zero, and the amount of radioactivity that could escape, if such an improbable event were to occur, is small enough to form only a minor and easily manageable public hazard. Of course, no such accidents have ever occurred since British Rail have been carrying these containers—a period of 20 years during which 4,500 journeys have taken place.

Similar arrangements have been made in the USA and it has been estimated that the risk of a radiation hazard from the transport of all the American radioactive materials by such means, is no more than might cause one death among 1,000 million million people, i.e. one person in 250,000 worlds with populations equal to the present one on earth.

To object to procedures as safe as these must raise serious doubts among sensible people about the judgement of those making the objections, and so thereby undermine the value, in the public's eye, of the protesters' arguments against much more significant nuclear hazards. It is foolish to cry wolf about every implausible possibility.

Safety against accidents

The basic principle of safe nuclear power is that radiation and radioactive materials should not be released from any nuclear plant to an extent which might harm anyone. Under normal running conditions the amounts released can be controlled, as we have seen, to levels well below the recommended ICRP limits. When an accident occurs, however, the sources of radioactive release may become *uncontrolled*; and if these are large sources, then there is the possibility of correspondingly large releases. This points to reprocessing plants and, still more, to the nuclear reactors themselves as the biggest potentially uncontrolled sources. An active reactor, containing some 10,000 million curies and a powerful energy source, e.g. 3,000 megawatts of heat, clearly has a latent capability of producing a serious accident.

For an uncontrolled release to occur on a large scale, a substantial mass of nuclear material has to *overheat* to such an extent that it melts, burns or vaporises. For this uncontrolled release to become a general hazard and public danger, a *pathway* has also to be opened up by which the released radioactive substances can pass from the source to the open environment. The analysis of nuclear safety is founded upon these two considerations. The first leads to the strict control of temperature as one method of providing safety; and of course temperature control is necessary also for the ordinary stable running of a nuclear plant. The second leads to an independent and supplementary method of providing safety by various kinds of *containment* and *isolation*, so as to prevent such pathways from opening up. At Three Mile Island the first method—temperature control—failed but the second—containment—succeeded. Thus there was little radioactivity released even though the interior of the reactor was partly wrecked by overheating.

There are three ways in which overheating can occur: by a *fire*, such as occurred at an early form of military reactor at Windscale in 1957; by an accidental increase in *nuclear reactivity*, for example taking a reactor up to the prompt critical state (see page 15); or by a reduction in the amount of *cooling* provided, for example due to the failure of a pump or a break in the coolant pipework. We will deal with fire hazards now, and look into the control of nuclear reactivity, and the possibility of loss-of-coolant accidents, in the next two chapters.

Fire hazards

The fire in the Windscale reactor was a serious accident which released about 20,000 curies of iodine–131 into the neighbouring countryside, so that it was necessary to stop milk supplies for a while from all farms in the affected area. There were no illnesses or casualties, however, and although the accident was rightly regarded as a matter of great public concern, it' did not set off the kind of general alarm experienced at Harrisburg.

Such a fire could not occur in any present-day power reactor, for two reasons. First, the early system of cooling the fuel rods by air, passed through the reactor along channels open to the *atmosphere*, is no longer used. All modern reactors are cooled by means of *closed circuits*, round which are passed coolants such as water, carbon dioxide or liquid metal. Second, the fire was brought about by an operation known as *releasing Wigner energy*, which is not required in modern reactors. The basis of this operation is as follows:

The collisions of neutrons with the carbon atoms of a graphite moderator not only slow the neutrons down, as required. They also cause the struck atoms to be *knocked out* of their normal positions in the graphite. As a result of this, the graphite gradually accumulates *stored energy* while it is in service in the reactor. If the temperature of the graphite is below about 100°C the amount of this stored energy can become quite large, sufficient if suddenly released to overheat the graphite to a temperature where, in an air-cooled reactor, it could begin to smoulder in the air passing through its fuel channels. This stored energy has therefore to be periodically released, by gently heating the reactor to a temperature well below the smouldering range, at which the knocked-on atoms could slowly slip back into place. It was during one of these Wigner releases, on 10 October 1957, that things went wrong. The deliberate heating was applied too vigorously, as a result of which the stored energy was released quickly, and the graphite overheated. The heat caused some of the fuel cans to split open, thereby exposing the uranium metal to the air, so that it began to oxidise sufficiently to raise the temperature still further and so to start a fuel channel fire.

The modern graphite-moderated power reactors do not need Wigner releases, because they operate at temperatures where the accumulation of stored energy in the graphite is very low.

There is in fact little scope for large conventional fires at modern thermal nuclear stations, for there is not much exposed flammable material in them. Nevertheless, occasional accidents do occur. A striking one happened to a reactor at Brown's Ferry, Alabama, in 1975. A workman, using a lighted candle to check the airflow in an electrical cable chamber below the control room, accidentally set fire to flammable packing material round the cables. The fire among the cables put some of the reactor's main safety control systems out of action, and a serious accident involving the public was only narrowly avoided.

Accidents due to conventional fires may occur of course at other nuclear plants. A recent example was that in the French reprocessing plant at Cap La Hague, near Cherbourg. Apparently a fire in the main transformer room caused a breakdown of the ventilation system, which provides an excess pressure in the buildings so that volatile nuclear materials cannot leak out of their chambers; and it also caused the pumps and cooling systems of the high-activity nuclear storage tanks to become switched off. As a result, there was some contamination of the plant itself, but not outside it.

One modern reactor which contains a lot of flammable material is the *liquid-sodium cooled fast breeder reactor* (LMFBR), mentioned in Chapter 2. The nuclear core of this reactor sits in a pool of about 1,000 tons of hot liquid sodium and the heat from this is conducted through a heat exchanger to a secondary liquid sodium system, which is circulated out to an external heat exchanger, where its heat raises steam for the turbines. Sodium burns in air and reacts energetically with water to form hydrogen and hydroxide. As regards burning, general industrial experience has shown that sodium burns with a smouldering slow fire which is not difficult to extinguish. The safety policy with the LMFBR is to avoid the possibility of such a fire, through the design of the plant, in particular by enclosing the primary sodium system in a double-walled vessel. Inside this, the sodium pool is kept under a cover of chemically inert argon gas. At the steam-raising heat exchanger, outside the reactor itself, the possibility of a leak which could allow sodium and water (steam) to meet has to be considered. A small leak would have a limited effect, because the hydrogen released *in situ* by the sodium-water reaction would push the reactants apart and so stifle the reaction. If there were a large leak, the sodium in the secondary circuit loop could be withdrawn quickly into a separate dump tank, provided for such an emergency. The primary sodium circuit has such a large capacity that, if a secondary circuit loop were lost, it could continue safely to absorb the residual heating from the shut-down nuclear core for several hours.

8

The control of nuclear reactivity

Criticality

For safe nuclear energy it is of utmost importance to keep the fission chain reaction under control at all times, otherwise destructively large amounts of energy may quickly appear. As we saw in Chapter 2, the stable running of a nuclear reactor is possible because some of the neutrons—needed for the continuation of the chain reaction – are emitted not promptly but only after times long enough to enable the neutron-absorbing control rods to be properly adjusted. The reactor is thus deliberately kept in a state of nuclear activity which is 'sub-critical' so far as the prompt neutrons alone are concerned (see page 15). It only becomes fully *critical*, i.e. reaches that threshold of nuclear activity at which a self-sustaining chain reaction is just possible, when *all* the neutrons, both prompt and delayed, play their part in the continuation of the reaction.

The nuclear reactivity of any mass of fissile material, whether in or out of a reactor, depends on many things—on the amount in the mass, on the size and shape of the mass (the sphere being the shape most conducive to reactivity), and on the presence of moderating substances, or neutron-absorbers, or a neutron reflector round the mass. It follows that extreme care must at all times be taken to avoid setting up a prompt critical or super-critical mass by accident. If this were to happen, for example in a fuel preparation or reprocessing plant, or in a nuclear materials store, the energy released would usually be sufficient to blow the critical mass apart and stop the reaction before it had gone very far; but, nevertheless, the gamma radiation and neutrons released even in this brief 'excursion' could be extremely dangerous to people working in the same building. Strict precautions are thus taken in nuclear plants to avoid accidentally bringing together such critical masses. Only a small amount of fissile material is allowed to be kept in any one place. Great care is taken to avoid the entrance into such places of water, or other moderating material, which could stimulate a nuclear reaction. At processing plants, where rich aqueous solutions of fissile material are handled, their chemical vessels are designed to have sizes and shapes that preclude criticality; and neutron-absorbing materials such as boron-steel are used in their construction.

The control of reactors

To start-up a reactor the first step is to provide a small source of neutrons within it. This releases a very small but definite 'primeval' population of neutrons in the core of the reactor. The fission process is then used to breed and multiply neutrons through several generations from this primeval population, so bringing the reactor up to the required full power. However, this multiplication of neutrons must be brought about only by allowing the reactor to exceed criticality slightly, i.e. by allowing more neutrons to be produced than consumed. During the earliest stages of start-up, while the neutron population is still very small, it is difficult to detect whether the reactor has gone into the prompt critical state. During the later stages, when the state of criticality becomes clear, there is not much time left to bring the reactor to stable running. As the power builds up, and especially as full power is approached, it is thus important to limit the reproduction of neutrons, including delayed ones, to the level at which the neutron population grows very slowly. Otherwise the reaction would be in danger of surging dangerously high if no further steps were taken.

For this reason the starting-up of a reactor is done very gradually, over many hours, by withdrawing the control rods in small and well separated steps, while monitoring at every stage the size of the neutron population, and other important indicators such as temperature. In addition, a second set of control rods—the *safety rods*—are held in reserve, above the reactor, in positions in which they can be instantly dropped into it, should an emergency arise. These safety rods are operated entirely independently of the control rods. They are released by signals from the monitoring instruments and work on a 'fail-safe' principle. For example, they may be held above the reactor by electromagnets which are switched off by warning signals from the monitors; and so, if the electricity supply to the magnets were to fail, they would drop down automatically, by gravity.

The nuclear activity of a reactor core depends not only on the position of the control rods. Some of the various fission products are strong neutron-absorbers and so reduce the activity, i.e. 'poison' the reactor. Moreover, because of changes which occur to these unstable products, transforming one isotope into another, the intensity of this poisoning can change with time even in a shut-down reactor. It has to be taken into account at all times during the working life of the reactor.

An important factor is *temperature*, which can alter the reactivity in various ways. Since increasing reactivity produces a higher temperature, the reactor designer does not want this increasing temperature to produce a higher reactivity in return, because that could lead to a vicious circle, i.e. to an *instability* in which initially trifling and almost unavoidable increases in reactivity and temperature would set each other off into an escalation. Instead, what is wanted is a *negative temperature coefficient* of reactivity, in which an increase of temperature causes a *lower* reactivity and so tends to *stabilise* the nuclear reaction at its designed level. Fortunately, because uranium−238 becomes a stronger neutron-absorber as it gets hotter, there is a very effective negative temperature coefficient built into all nuclear fuel which contains a large proportion of this uranium isotope. We saw the importance of this for the safe running of a fast reactor, at the end of Chapter 2. A valuable feature of this negative fuel temperature coefficient, which is also present in thermal uranium reactors, is that it applies as soon as the change in fuel temperature occurs and so opposes a reactivity change immediately one begins.

In a thermal reactor, an increase in the temperature of the *moderator* also in some circumstances leads to a negative temperature coefficient. Water is better than graphite in this respect. However, when the thermal reactor fuel contains more than a certain amount of plutonium−239 the position changes, because this isotope is particularly easily fissioned by higher-temperature thermal neutrons. In this situation a graphite moderator can provide a *positive* temperature coefficient. (The temperature coefficient of the fuel continues, of course, to be negative.) However, because the moderator has a large heat-absorbing capacity and is separated from the fuel by the coolant channels, its temperature rises only slowly. Accordingly there is plenty of time to take correcting action and stabilise the reactor against the effect of the positive moderator temperature coefficient. In a graphite-moderated reactor, the temperature is measured at various points throughout the core, and the signals from the measuring instruments set small motors going which move the control rods slightly in or out, so compensating for the effect of graphite temperature on reactivity.

Changes in the structure of the core

Ideally, the fuel rods, moderator and coolant are arranged in that configuration which is most conducive to nuclear reactivity. As well as its obvious economic advantages—in using least material to generate a given output—this configuration also provides an important safety feature in that, if such a core were to be suddenly collapsed by some serious accident, its pieces could not then fall into a *more* reactive configuration. The chain reaction would thus shut down in a randomised structure.

Thermal reactors generally do have this natural safety feature, although they do not rely on it, but also have safety rods and other shut-down systems to deal with emergencies. The general safety principle is that, if something goes seriously wrong in a reactor, the nuclear reaction must without fail immediately be shut down by the various safety devices provided. For example, although a reactor is pretty resistant to external shocks such as earthquakes, aircraft crashes or nearby explosions—because of its massive and thick concrete construction—nevertheless one safety practice is to provide boron-steel neutron-absorbing balls, which can be released to drop into the core by gravity should the normal control and safety rod channels in some way become closed or distorted.

The cores of thermal reactors can be, and are, designed to have very nearly the ideal configuration for greatest reactivity. In a graphite reactor, major changes of configuration are simply prevented by the solid mass of the moderator itself. In water-moderated reactors such changes could in principle occur, but in almost all cases they would lead to a drop in reactivity. If the fuel rods somehow became closely bunched together or collapsed into a dense mass, the separation of interior parts of the fuel from the moderator would then reduce the reaction. Moreover, if the water boiled and vapour bubbles formed around the fuel, the moderating of the neutrons would thereby be diminished and this also would reduce the reactivity. Liquid water thus has a *negative void coefficient* of reactivity; in other words, a bubble in liquid water is a wasted space in the moderator, in which no significant moderation takes place.

In the *pressurised water reactor* (PWR) the water is held under very high pressure in completely liquid form, even at the full operating temperature. If something were to go wrong and cause the water to vaporise, the nuclear reaction would on this account be shut down—although the reactor does not rely on this safety feature because (as we shall see in the next chapter) cooling water must be supplied to the reactor at all times to keep the fuel from overheating. The other type of light-water reactor is the *boiling water reactor* (BWR), in which the water in the core is allowed to boil and the steam from it led out to turbines. If, as occasionally happens, one of the electrical generators is shut down, the reaction of its turbine produces an increased pressure in the reactor. This can collapse the steam bubbles and so increase the reactivity. The reactor relies on the certainty and speed of action of its automatic safety rods system for protection against such a surge of reactivity.

Criticality in the fast reactor

A fast reactor has no moderator. Furthermore, the liquid sodium used to cool it is a weak absorber of the fast neutrons which keep its chain reaction going. As a result, if the fuel happened for some reason to slump down or to melt into a compact mass from which liquid sodium was largely excluded, there would be an *increase* in nuclear reactivity. Similarly, the liquid sodium has a *positive void coefficient*. In other words, if bubbles form in it, then the lack of neutron absorber in those spaces in the coolant enables the nuclear reaction to go ahead more energetically.

While such a reactivity surge is a very important possibility, against which special measures are taken, it could not bring the reactor up to the prompt critical state. This is for the reason given earlier (Chapter 2), that the uranium−238 in the fuel absorbs more neutrons as it gets hotter. Compared with the timescale of nuclear fission and the heating of the fuel which immediately follows it, the mechanical collapse of the core and the vaporisation of sodium are rather slow processes. As a result, the temperature starts rising as soon as these changes begin; and the strongly negative temperature coefficient of the fuel then brings the reactivity under control. The mechanical collapse or vaporisation may of course still continue, with more heating of the fuel and consequential control of the reactivity. As a result, the reactivity cannot increase in such accidents by very much; and the main outcome, from the safety point of view, is the large increase in temperature which may occur. This increase, if it goes through to the stage of a major disruption of the core, will also close down the nuclear reaction by sweeping the molten fuel upwards and outwards in the stream of sodium bubbling up from the core.

Not surprisingly, a great deal of work has gone into security and protection against such accidents. Various measures are taken to prevent them. In addition to these, a large *containment vessel*, which we shall discuss in Chapter 10, is provided to resist the energy released by such an eruption of the core and to prevent radioactive substances escaping into the atmosphere. For such an accident to occur at all, it would be necessary to have *two* preceding major faults—a large-scale loss of flow of sodium coolant into the reactor and thereafter a failure of the automatic safety devices. The design of the reactor, in which the core sits at the bottom of a large pool of sodium—the natural convection of which is sufficient to keep the coolant moving through the core—is intended to make the first of these practically impossible. So far as the second is concerned, an extremely reliable system of safety control rods is provided. Typically there are about 30 of these, which use more than one design and mode of operation; and if only five of them work, that is sufficient to shut down the fission reaction.

9

Keeping cool

Choosing a coolant

We come now to the third way in which overheating can occur: by loss of coolant. The *nuclear heating* obviously has to be kept under strict control at all times, in a reactor. But this is only one of the requirements for reactor safety. Equally important is the need to ensure that this heat is unfailingly removed from the reactor, so that the *temperature* is also kept under strict control. The reactor *coolant* together with all its equipment—vessels, pipes, pumps, valves, meters, pressure gauges, etc.—is thus much more than merely the means by which the energy is taken from the reactor core out to the heat exchangers and electrical turbo-generators. It is, second only to the nuclear controls themselves, the most important feature of the reactor for stability and safety.

Moreover, this safety role of the coolant continues even when the reactor is shut down and there is no more fission heating. After it has been running for some time, a reactor contains a lot of unstable nuclei. The radioactive changes which go on in these nuclei, over various times related to their half-lives, provide the reactor with a large amount of *decay heat* even after the fission reaction has been shut down. Immediately after shut-down, this heat is about 6 to 7 per cent of the preceding fission heating. For example a 1,000 megawatt (electrical) reactor, which produces about 3,000 megawatts of fission heating, even when shut down continues initially to produce about 200 megawatts of decay heating. This is equivalent to having 200,000 domestic electric fires switched on inside the reactor vessel! This decay heat must be removed by the coolant, if the reactor is not to overheat and become a safety hazard when shut down. As the radioactive changes take place and the unstable nuclei progressively change into stable nuclei, so the decay heating gradually diminishes. But even after many weeks it is still appreciable and has to be removed.

Although several substances have promising qualities as reactor coolants, especially *helium* gas and certain *organic* liquids, the three main coolants today are *water, carbon dioxide* and *sodium*.The first two are already used in standard thermal nuclear power stations and the third, liquid sodium, is the coolant used in the liquid-metal cooled fast breeder reactor (LMFBR). The choice of coolant very largely determines the main features of a reactor, so that reactors are commonly named from their coolants, e.g. *light-water, heavy-water, gas-cooled* and *liquid-metal* reactors.

Low-intensity reactors

Water is both a coolant and a moderator (see page 12), and modern water reactors use it for both purposes. By contrast, gas-cooled thermal reactors use a separate moderator, a large stack of graphite blocks; and in fast reactors there is of course no moderator. Because of its low density a gas is generally not so good at transferring heat as a liquid. For this reason—and also because the relatively heavy carbon atoms of a graphite moderator absorb less neutron energy, per collision, than the light hydrogen atoms of water, so that a large mass of graphite moderator is needed, with well-spaced fuel channels—a gas-cooled graphite reactor is a large object. Its nuclear core is about the size of an average house.

Although a disadvantage from the economic point of view, this large core is a valuable safety feature because, for a given total output of power from the reactor, the *density* of power output from any small part of it is fairly low—not more than about 4.5 kilowatts per litre— much smaller in fact than in other types of reactor. The gas-graphite reactor is thus a big *low-intensity* reactor. The demands it makes on the coolant are lower than for any other. Moreover, the mass of graphite serves as a huge heat absorber. If the coolant were to fail, the decay heating could not raise the graphite temperature by more than about 2°C a minute.

For somewhat different reasons, heavy-water reactors also have this safety feature. Heavy water is valued as a moderator particularly because it *absorbs* very few neutrons. In its ability to *slow down* neutrons it is, while better than graphite, much inferior to light water because its hydrogen−2 nuclei absorb less energy per collision than the hydrogen−1 nuclei of light water. Thus, a heavy-water moderator has to be fairly large, about the size of a small cottage, and the power density is again fairly low, only a few times higher than that of a gas-graphite power reactor. Moreover, heavy water performs best when cool. For this reason, the Canadian Candu reactor uses a large bath of cold heavy water for its moderator, through which pass a number of metal *pressure tubes*. These pressure tubes carry a flow of heavy water coolant past the fuel element rods, which are located along the centre of these tubes. This large bath of cold water thus serves as a safety feature, in being able to cool the fuel should there be a major break-down of the pressure tubes.

High-intensity reactors

Light water is the most effective moderator, although it also absorbs neutrons fairly strongly. The fuel rods are thus set close together in a light-water reactor and the whole core is very compact, about the size of a little room. The power density is then high, about 50 to 100 kilowatts per litre, so that the reactor has a *high intensity*. Although water can absorb much heat by boiling, its conversion to steam largely destroys its coolant properties as well as creating huge volumes of vapour. An imperative feature of a light-water reactor therefore is that the fuel rods of the core should be flooded at all times, during and after the use of the reactor, with liquid coolant. A special *emergency core-cooling system* (ECCS) is provided for this purpose.

Liquid sodium, because of its exceptionally high heat conductivity due to its metallic nature, is an extremely powerful coolant. For this reason, and because no moderator is required, the LMFBR core is very compact, being not much larger than a big domestic hot water tank, and it generates an immense power density, about 400 kilowatts per litre. This is an enormously concentrated energy source. But it must be judged against the equally enormous capacity to remove and absorb heat of the sodium pool—at the bottom of which the reactor core sits. Experiments on the prototype fast reactor at Dounreay in Scotland have in fact shown that, once the shut-down control rods are inserted, the liquid sodium is able to cool the reactor safely by *natural circulation*, due to pure convection, even when all the coolant pumps are switched off. The cooling power of this natural process is sufficient to remove much more than the full decay heat of the reactor.

Safety problems with coolants

Water, carbon dioxide and sodium have several properties important for the safety of reactors. They are all chemically reactive, especially at high temperatures. This not only dictates the choice of other materials used in reactors, which need to be chemically compatible with the coolants—for example, fuel cans are made of *zirconium* in water reactors, of *magnesium* alloy in the early (Magnox) gas-cooled reactors and of *stainless steel* in the later (AGR) reactors and also in the LMFBR—it also leads to various corrosion and oxidation effects, particularly on graphite and on the metal cooling circuits. Various steps are taken to deal with these. If not checked, these effects can lead to the gradual deterioration and hence to the more restricted use or even early retirement of reactors. Furthermore, they set some safety problems. A few years ago several BWRs had to be closed down for inspection and repair because chloride impurity in water was found to be causing cracks, by stress-corrosion, in stainless steel cooling circuit pipes. At about the same time the carbon dioxide coolant in the earlier Magnox reactors was discovered to be oxidising the steel bolts of the type then used in those reactors; in case this might cause difficulties with the mechanisms of the standard shut-down devices, a precautionary system was fitted which relied simply upon boron steel balls falling into the reactor core.

The main safety problems of the coolants come not from chemistry, however, but physics. It matters very much whether the coolant is a *liquid* or *gas*; and whether it can change from one of those states to the other, in the reactor. For example, *sodium* has an important advantage over the other coolants in that, at *atmospheric pressure*, it remains a liquid over the whole range of normal temperatures of the LMFBR. It does not solidify until cooled below 100°C or boil until heated up to nearly 900°C, which is well above the temperature (575°C) at which it is called upon to carry the heat out of the reactor. Because of this, the LMFBR does not have to be kept under high pressure. This simplifies the design and operation of the reactor and, more importantly, avoids the need for a *pressure vessel* and the various safety problems which centre round the possibilities of *depressurisation* accidents and sudden loss of coolant. Once the shut-down rods are in, the LMFBR becomes completely safe. It does not require power to pressurise its coolant and could simply be left unattended for many hours. Pressurised reactors, by contrast, still need external actions for their safety even when shut down.

Carbon dioxide is always a *gas*, under all reactor conditions, and this gives it important safety advantages over the liquid coolants, water and sodium. As a gas it retains its same physical state and properties under all circumstances. It spreads evenly throughout its container so that there is never any doubt about where it is: it is everywhere, equally. It obeys a very reliable law of nature which relates its pressure simply and directly to its temperature. Unlike water, it cannot change its state and lose its coolant properties in a depressurisation accident, and it raises no problems of cavitation which could leave the fuel elements inadequately cooled or the circulating pumps without a working fluid. Moreover, when a gas-cooled reactor is shut down it can be brought quickly to atmospheric pressure, unlike a water reactor where the pressure has to be kept on for a long time afterwards in order to hold the water as liquid at temperatures above 100°C.

Finally, because it is already a gas, carbon dioxide is unlike sodium and water in that it cannot raise the hazard of *boiling* in a bad accident where the core becomes greatly overheated. Any reactor with a liquid coolant poses the possibility that if the fuel were to melt, at a temperature above the boiling point of the coolant, it could cause the coolant to vaporise suddenly and so set off a *vapour explosion* that might blow the core apart. This is an unlikely event in the LMFBR and even less likely in a water reactor, but it cannot be entirely ruled out. Experiments in which molten uranium oxide fuel has been poured into molten sodium have in fact *not* produced vapour explosions. This may be due to the very high heat conductivity of sodium preventing the metal next to the fuel from vapourising, or else to the release of gases from the fuel which form an insulating jacket between it and the sodium. Nevertheless, the possibility of a vapour explosion still remains, in principle at least, and has to be guarded against by means of an exceptionally secure set of detecting and emergency shut-down devices.

To do its job as a reactor coolant, carbon dioxide has to be used under pressure—up to 25 atmospheres in Magnox reactors and 40 atm in AGRs—and so a pressure vessel and circuit are necessary. The most serious type of accident envisaged for such a reactor is in fact a *depressurisation*, a rapid loss of coolant due for example to a fracture of a pipe in the cooling circuit. However, if the shut-down rods go in promptly, enough gas can then be kept circulating *even at atmospheric pressure* to cool the fuel and prevent the escape of all but a trace of radioactive substances. A very secure shut-down system is provided, through a large number of automatic safety rods which operate by different methods so as to avoid an unforeseen fault common to all. Emergency supplies of carbon dioxide are also kept ready, to be fed into the circuit and so prevent air entering. Experiments have shown that the temperature in gas-cooled reactors does not go very high when there is a sudden loss of coolant pressure. It rises at first, but not beyond the range at which the fuel cladding is safe, and it falls back again once an auxiliary gas flow is brought into action.

Water is only a good coolant so long as it remains liquid. As steam it is much less effective. A prime requirement in water reactors, then, is that the fuel rods must be surrounded with liquid water at all times. However, if this same water is also to be the carrier of the heat from an efficient power producer, it has to be heated far above 100°C, its ordinary boiling point. In fact, the outlet coolant temperatures in water reactors all lie in the range of 300°C. These two requirements are reconciled by keeping the water under *high pressure*, i.e. at about 70 atmospheres in BWR, 85 in Candu and 150 in PWR. Because of this, a highly-stressed pressure circuit has to be used in all these reactors, which raises various safety problems concerned with the possibilities of depressurisation and loss of coolant. Even when such a reactor is shut down the water pressure cannot be taken off until much later, only after the decay heat has diminished far enough to bring the water temperature below 100°C.

Minor incidents such as failures of valves to close can grow into major ones if they lead to a loss of pressure and the water turns into steam. There can then be local or general boiling, trapped steam pockets, overheating of fuel rods exposed to steam and loss of action from dry pumps. The reactor operators may not have good information about the amount of water in the system—as happened at Three Mile Island—and so may be misled into making wrong diagnoses and mistakes. If there is a major depressurisation, for example due to a large break in the pressure circuit, the water can 'flash' and 'blow-down' rapidly into steam, releasing a lot of energy in so doing. The exposed fuel rods then heat up rapidly, and if they are not quickly flooded with cooling water they may become too hot for water cooling, and will be set to melt from their decay heating. The reason is that when the zirconium cladding gets very hot it becomes oxidised from the oxygen of the water. The hydrogen which is then left floats off and forms a hydrogen 'bubble' above the core, as happened so notably at Three Mile Island. This oxidation releases chemical heat and, when the zirconium becomes extremely hot, this is sufficient to make water a *heater* of the cladding, not a coolant.

For all these reasons an emergency core cooling system (ECCS), which will act quickly and automatically whenever called upon to do so, is an absolutely essential safety requirement of a water reactor. At Three Mile Island it came into operation automatically, soon after the start of the incident, exactly as intended. Unfortunately it was then switched off a few minutes later by the operators, in the mistaken belief that the reactor was too full of water. The fuel rods were then left without water for some hours and the accident thus moved into a more dangerous phase, with fuel temperatures going high enough to create a large amount of hydrogen by the zirconium reaction. Nevertheless, the even worse disaster of the melting of the fuel through the bottom of the steel pressure vessel and down into the ground below—the notorious *China syndrome*—did *not* occur. This at least was one encouraging result from the accident; but whether the China syndrome could have occurred if circumstances had been slightly different or whether steam, poor coolant though it is, was nevertheless able to carry enough heat away to prevent it, is not clear.

Emergency core cooling

Because of the vital role which it has to play in a loss-of-coolant accident, caused for example by a broken pipe or failed valve, the emergency core cooling system (ECCS) of a water reactor is designed to be a highly reliable set of devices for injecting water into the reactor to reflood the entire core. In the PWR for example *all* pipes leading into the reactor join it *above* the core, so that there is no possibility of the core being left exposed by a leak below it (unless the pressure vessel itself breaks, at some lower point). The reactor has three emergency cooling systems. One is simply a large reservoir of water held above the reactor, which can be piped down into the core when needed. The other two are a *low-pressure* pumped system for incidents in which there is a large depressurisation, and a *high-pressure* pumped system for those in which the pressure remains high. These systems are set up to operate automatically and immediately, upon command from various monitoring instruments.

While these arrangements seem very secure—although not proof against mistaken actions by reactor operators, as was shown at Three Mile Island—they nevertheless have been a centre of controversy. The doubt has been over whether the ECCS water will actually get to the fuel rods, because it may be forced back by the pressure of steam issuing from the core itself, or pushing backwards from broken exchangers. Or it may be side-tracked into spilling out through the broken pipe, or other opening in the primary coolant circuit which caused the depressurisation. Furthermore, the overheated fuel rods may have become so swollen and distorted as to block some of the water passages between them; and their surfaces may have become so hot and dry that a stable insulating film of steam is formed along them. Certainly, in the early stages of reflooding an exposed and very hot core, the cooling has to be done by a mixture of steam and water, the cooling properties of which are scientifically complex and not well understood. Model tests have been studied and computer simulations calculated, but uncertainties remain. As a result, the US Atomic Energy Commission a few years ago increased their demanded factor of safety, so that some reactors were required to run at lower power or use a smaller diameter of fuel rod, in order to limit the maximum possible temperature of the fuel rods. Most, but not all, of the independent experts have accepted that this provides an adequate level of safety.

Pressure vessels

Thermal reactors are pressurised, and the envisaged starting point for the worst kinds of accidents in these reactors is a depressurisation, due to a sudden break somewhere in a pressure circuit. We have already discussed methods for dealing with breakages in the pipework of the pressure circuit, i.e. the application of emergency nuclear shut-down devices and the control of the decay heating: in gas-graphite reactors by cooling at atmospheric pressure, and in water reactors by ECCS. We now have to consider the security of the pressure vessels which enclose the nuclear core itself. In most thermal reactors these are large heavy envelopes of highly-stressed material, surrounding the entire reactor core. A sudden and major break in one of these could produce an accident of immense ferocity, with loss of coolant, breakdown of most controls, possible destruction of the outer reactor building by large flying pieces and exposure of the core to the general environment. The security of the pressure vessel is thus of overriding importance for the safety of a thermal nuclear reactor.

The high working stresses in a pressure vessel come of course from the expansive force exerted by the compressed coolant in the vessel. The design of the vessel, and the choice of the material used, are naturally such that in normal circumstances these stresses can be carried with a wide margin of safety. They fall well below the strength of the material. The problem is whether this strength is likely to be undermined in any way, for example by effects of heat and radiation on the material, or ageing and corrosion; and above all by the presence and growth of *cracks* in the material. It is well known from engineering experience, and well understood scientifically, that the more deeply a sharp crack penetrates into a vessel wall, of a given material under a given stress, the easier it is for that crack to penetrate still further. In many constructional materials there is a critical stage, at a certain depth of penetration, at which a crack becomes unstable and will then run on rapidly in the material, at almost the speed of sound, to rip the material completely apart in a fraction of a second. It is this *fast fracture* which must at all costs be avoided.

There are several ways of achieving this. One way is provided by the *leak-before-break* principle. In this the design and material of the vessel are so chosen that the *critical crack size*, i.e. that depth at which a growing crack is able to turn into a fast fracture, is safely *larger* than the wall thickness of the vessel. In these circumstances any crack which is too small to penetrate right through the vessel wall is also much too small to grow rapidly. Furthermore if it then grows slowly it will *perforate* the wall, and so announce its presence through a small *leaking* of the vessel. This leak can easily be detected and remedial action taken, long before it has grown to the dangerous critical size. This principle is followed in the Candu reactor. Here the pressure 'vessel' consists of a large number of separate zirconium *pressure tubes*, which pass horizontally through the heavy-water tank. Each tube, which carries one line of fuel rods, is about 4 inches diameter and has a wall thickness of about 0.2 inches. The mechanical conditions of the zirconium are such that the critical crack size is about 4 inches, i.e. very much larger than the wall thickness. The design of the reactor makes it fairly easy to remove a defective tube and replace it with a sound one. The large steel pressure vessels which surround the graphite cores of the early low-pressure Magnox reactors, and which have wall thicknesses of about 3 inches, also satisfy the leak-before-break principle, although more marginally.

Reinforced-concrete pressure vessels are used in all the later gas-cooled reactors. Here the safety principle is quite different; it is to avoid having a *continuous* material in which an uninterrupted progress of a crack is possible. The forces from the gas pressure are carried in these vessels by large numbers of steel cables, threaded through channels in the concrete. Failure of a single cable does not cause the whole vessel to break, but it gives a significant early warning of conditions in the vessel. Each cable can be inspected and replaced, if necessary, at any time during the life of the reactor. An additional safety advantage of large reinforced-concrete pressure vessels is that it is possible to house, not only the reactor core, but also the boilers and the pipework joining them, all within the overall protection of the vessel.

The light-water reactors, PWR and BWR, rely on neither of these methods. In both of these the reactor core is enclosed in a massive steel pressure vessel consisting of a round upright cylinder, about 14 ft in diameter and 40 ft high, with rounded ends. The walls are very thick, typically 8 inches or so, and even thicker round the pipe openings. This great thickness is necessary to withstand the very high water pressures without overstressing the steel. A leak-before-break cannot be guaranteed in this case. The security of these thick steel vessels thus depends on the *avoidance* of dangerously large cracks or similar defects in the metal. The first step is to choose a type of steel tough enough to resist the quick spreading of all but the very largest cracks. PWR steel is such that cracks less than about 4 inches deep would not set off fast fracture under ordinary operating conditions[1]. This seems safe enough, but we have to consider also the more severe conditions to which the steel can be subjected when there is a major fault, such as the breaking of a steam line or an accident involving loss of coolant. In fact, in these circumstances the ensuing changes of temperature and pressure can reduce the critical crack size down to not much more than 1 inch in certain cases[1]. Now, while high-quality steel manufacturing and welding processes should normally be able to avoid introducing 1 inch cracks in the material, this cannot be absolutely guaranteed, especially in pieces as thick as those for PWR vessels. It follows that, although the very best manufacturing practices obviously have to be applied, these must be supplemented by an *inspection procedure*, to make sure that no cracks of dangerous size have been left in the metal, or develop in it during service.

The most important inspection procedure is by *ultrasonics*, a kind of sonar method which finds cracks inside the metal by the echoes from them of high-frequency sound waves injected through the surface. In principle the method could detect cracks down to 0.1 inch, but in practice this is hardly possible because it is rather like trying to peer into a turbid river to see the stones on the bed below. A special problem exists near the inner surface of the pressure vessel where a layer of stainless steel cladding acts as a kind of mirror, reflecting the sound waves and so obscuring the view of defects immediately below the surface. In fact, tests of the best standard ultrasonic practice on thick steel plate have shown that there is a mere *half* chance of detecting even a one inch crack[2]. Only cracks deeper than about 2 inches have a high (e.g. better than 95%) probability of being detected. Clearly, *an improvement in ultrasonic techniques and procedures, to well beyond the best standard practice, is required if all potentially dangerous cracks are to be detected*. A minimum goal here ought to be the proven ability in practice to detect ¼ inch cracks with a fair (e.g. 50%) probability and 1 inch cracks with very high (better than 95%) probability.

One-quarter inch cracks are well below the dangerous range, provided that the vessel has been made to specification and provided that it is not highly stressed when cold. Nevertheless, such cracks are still significant for two reasons. First there is the possibility that, during the life of the reactor, they may slowly grow deeper, particularly by metal fatigue accentuated by corrosion, and so may eventually become dangerously large. The second point is that ¼ inch is about the greatest

10

Defence in depth

The significance of melting

Like any large and complicated piece of engineering, a nuclear reactor can in principle go wrong in many different ways. Mostly these are minor malfunctions, easily overcome. A few are serious. Large operational safety manuals are written which analyse a multitude of conceivable faults in detail; and these have of course to be thoroughly understood and acted upon, by the operators, for the good running and general protection of the plant. There is a great economic incentive for this, quite apart from the need to protect the operators and the general public.

So far as public safety is concerned, what particularly distinguishes the serious from the minor accidents is the *melting* of the fuel, or the possibility of its melting. All those malfunctions which do not bring this about are of little more significance, in their effect on the public, than small everyday industrial accidents. The risk to the public becomes serious only when a large part of the fuel melts or becomes likely to do so. The reason is that most of the atoms responsible for the radioactive hazard in a reactor stay close to where they were created, inside the solid fuel or its enveloping can of cladding material. Once a radioactive atom has come to rest, after its creation, it is almost immobile inside a solid, being trapped in place by the densely packed and strongly bonded atoms of the material itself. But if the fuel melts, and if its can also fails—for example by bursting, melting or oxidising —then the mobility of the liquid gives the atoms plenty of freedom to move about. A large number, perhaps a tenth, of the volatile radioactive atoms could then escape into the coolant.

A natural defence against the large-scale release of radioactivity is therefore provided by the *solidity* and *continuity* of the fuel and of the metallic can in which it is sealed. So long as these remain intact, little radioactivity can escape. A good feature here is that the fuel used in most modern reactors consists of *uranium dioxide* (together with plutonium oxide in fast reactors) and this is an extremely stable and refractory substance with a melting point of about 2,800°C. Moreover, the melting points of the canning materials—zirconium alloy (about 1,800°C) and stainless steel (about 1,500°C)—are also fairly high. The Magnox reactors use materials which are less refractory—uranium metal (about 1,135°C) and magnesium alloy (about 650°C). But a compensating factor here is the low power density, only about 1 kilowatt per litre, which enables gas cooling even at atmospheric pressure to control temperatures due to decay heating.

Prevention of melt-downs

To avoid the possibility of a melt-down, the obvious first defence is to use extremely high standards of design, construction, inspection and operation, so that there is little chance of things going wrong. Naturally, all reactor specifications demand such standards. Although the quality of reactor engineering is very high, therefore, there is nonetheless always some possibility of human error creeping in. An absolutely immaculate standard in practice is unattainable. The occasional faulty item will slip through, or be put together badly, and not always be detected. An occasional mistake will sometimes be made in running the reactor—a wrongly closed valve, a false reading on an instrument, an ill-judged action. And so a further line of defence is necessary, in case an important fault develops despite the generally high engineering and operational standards. This further defence consists of various protective devices designed to take control of the faulty reactor and bring it to complete safety. An independent system of alternative power for circulating the coolant and activating the reactor controls is one obvious example. Others include the various independent emergency nuclear shut-down devices, and the emergency core cooling systems.

Defence in depth, therefore, results from the requirement that at least *two* independent major functions have to go wrong, at the same time, for a melt-down. As well as the original fault in the normal operating system, there has also to be a failure of an essential protective system for controlling this fault. Given the high standard of engineering, so that the probability of either going wrong is very small, and given a design and mode of operation which ensures that they are truly independent—in the sense that a fault in one cannot induce a fault in the other—then the chance of *both* going wrong at the same time is extremely small.

This is a good safety principle, but it has limitations. For example, although the two systems may be mechanically independent, they are nevertheless coupled together in the *mind* of the reactor operator. Through his attempts to manage the crisis, by taking charge of the controls manually, the fault in the normal system may influence the protective system. This happened at Three Mile Island. When the reactor suffered a loss-of-coolant fault as a result of a stuck valve, the operators were unfortunately led, from misleading instruments, to throttle down the emergency core cooling system, in the mistaken belief that the reactor was too full of water.

In a thermal reactor, a further point is that if a depressurisation occurs leading to a loss of coolant, then *two* protective systems— nuclear shut-down and emergency core cooling—have *both* to work properly if the fuel is not to overheat. The nuclear shut-down is of course extremely important, since it immediately cuts off about 94 percent of the heating and removes the risk of prompt criticality. For this reason, a most elaborate defence in depth is provided, with several shut-down systems working independently on different principles, each able by itself to shut the reactor down. It is virtually impossible for all of these to fail.

The core cooling is not technically demanding in gas-cooled reactors, because the core heats up quite slowly when there is a loss of coolant, and because all that is needed to control this heating is a circulation of coolant at atmospheric pressure. In high-intensity, high-pressure and quick-changing light water reactors, the ECCS is technically more demanding and difficult. Protection against serious overheating accidents is in fact more difficult in water than in gas-cooled reactors, and for this reason they are given an extra layer of *containment* (discussed below) to limit the consequences of a melt-down.

Even where general cooling is fully kept going, it is still possible to have a *local* loss of coolant through a *blockage* at a coolant inlet, caused for example by broken pieces of graphite at the bottom of a fuel channel in a gas-cooled reactor. In fact, this happened in an early Magnox reactor, at Chapelcross, Scotland, in 1967. As a result, the magnesium alloy cladding and some uranium in one channel melted through local overheating, due to a reduction of coolant flow in that channel. The reactor was immediately shut down and no radioactivity escaped. While this was a serious accident for the reactor itself, which had then to be taken out of service for two years for repairs, the relatively minor releases into the coolant from one melted channel were satisfactorily held within the pressure vessel and circuit. In consequence, there was no public hazard.

The one kind of failure which at a stroke could breach all these defences is a sudden major rupture of the pressure vessel. This would almost certainly take the reactor to disaster in a single instant step. Complete depressurisation and loss of coolant would probably be accompanied by a disabling of the shut-down and emergency cooling systems, together with a violent expansion of the depressurised coolant, with large pieces of the vessel being thrown apart. The security of the pressure vessel against such a catastrophic rupture is thus an absolutely essential safety requirement of a thermal reactor. We have seen in the last chapter the advantages of the reinforced-concrete type of vessel in which sudden rapid fracture is not possible; and also those of the Candu pressure-tube system in which the 'pressure vessel' is dispersed in the form of a large number of separate tubes, the failure of any one of which would produce only a small and easily containable accident.

So far as the liquid-metal fast breeder reactor is concerned, when something goes wrong the shut-down systems must jump into action with certainty, the instant they are required. In other respects the LMFBR differs greatly from thermal reactors in regard to the prevention of melt-down. Its coolant is virtually guaranteed at all times, the core being at the bottom of a large unpressurised pool of sodium, supported by a large and secure concrete vault. The sodium has a high heat conductivity, large heat capacity, and is liquid at atmospheric pressure up to temperatures well above the normal operating range. All the depressurisation problems and ECCS requirements thus vanish for this reactor. Even the stand-by sodium pumps with independent power supplies, although provided, are not strictly essential since natural circulation of the sodium is very effective in removing heat.

The main problem with the LMFBR is the possibility of a local blockage near one of the sodium inlets at the bottom of the core. This could lead to a rapid heating of those fuel rods starved of coolant by the blockage. Unlike the case of the gas-cooled reactor, where the fuel channels are isolated from each other by thick blocks of graphite, the overheating of a local part of the core in a fast reactor could quickly affect other nearby parts and so produce a larger failure. The prevention of local blockage is thus particularly important in this case. Blockage due to debris in the sodium is virtually eliminated by strict control of the purity of the coolant and by suitable design of the coolant inlets and filters. But a local blockage could be caused by the overheating of a fuel rod, for any reason whatsoever, leading to the distortion of its can. The early stages of this overheating and local failure can be detected by several different kinds of instruments, which monitor various parts of the core and activate the shut-down system. A local blockage produces only a small region of boiling sodium (which can be detected by acoustic monitors) because the interconnection of the coolant channels enables liquid sodium to flow across from neighbouring channels.

The general conditions for the prevention of a melt-down can thus be put very simply in the case of an LMFBR. First, it must always be possible to shut-down the reactor when required. Second, there must always be a reliable set of signals, monitoring local conditions throughout the core, which are capable of triggering the shut-down devices on any signs of incipient failure anywhere in the core.

Containment of the effects of melt-downs

The principle of defence in depth requires not only defences to prevent melt-downs from occurring, but also other, quite separate, defences to limit the consequences should a melt-down occur. These are of two kinds: *containment* and *isolation*. The aim in containment is to erect, between the reactor core and the outside world, barriers which are both strong enough to resist the forces from accidental releases of energy, and continuous enough to hold in the radioactive substances. The pressure vessel and circuit of a thermal reactor provide one such barrier. Some types of reactor in fact are enclosed in a strong *containment building*. The main challenge to such barriers comes from a melt-down. As well as immediately releasing radioactivity into the coolant, this could in extreme cases cause liquid coolant to vaporise, perhaps even explosively, and the fuel could melt through the bottom of the reactor (i.e. the China syndrome). Other effects could also occur such as the formation of hydrogen—which in fact caused a minor explosion in the Three Mile Island containment building—due to the chemical reaction between hot zirconium and water.

All civil reactors are provided with containment. But there is a significant difference between fast and thermal reactors, due to the pressurisation of the latter. The containment envelopes round a LMFBR are purely safety features, with no ordinary operational role. By contrast, the pressure vessel and circuit of a thermal reactor is only *secondarily* a safety feature. Its main purpose is to hold the coolant under pressure. The possibility, however remote, of its failing to do this makes it a safety *hazard*, as well as a safety feature. Water reactors in fact have an *additional* outer containment building which is a pure safety feature.

The plans for the commercial LMFBR include two containment envelopes. There is first an inner reinforced-concrete pressure vessel round the core and coolant, designed to withstand temperatures and pressures from a melt-down which disrupts the core. Secondly, there is an outer containment building, intended to catch any radioactivity which might slowly leak out of the primary containment after an accident.

A great advantage of reinforced-concrete pressure vessels, of the type used in the later Magnox reactors and all AGRs, is that they can be made very large and massive. They can be so large, in fact, that the *entire* reactor coolant circuit—the core, pipework and boilers—can all be contained inside the pressure vessel. This is a very safe arrangement, especially as the structure of the pressure vessel is one in which a sudden, catastrophic failure is virtually impossible.

As we have seen, the integrity of the pressure circuit in a water reactor cannot be so easily guaranteed. For this reason, all PWR, BWR and CANDU reactors have outer containment buildings. The PWR building, for example, consists of reinforced concrete lined with steel, and is tested up to a pressure of about five atmospheres which is well above the successfully-contained pressure pulse (about two atmospheres) produced by the hydrogen explosion in the Three Mile Island building. It is not clear, however, whether such a building could withstand a more violent explosion, such as would occur if for example the steel pressure vessel suddenly broke while the reactor was under power. Various devices are arranged inside the containment building to control releases of steam and radioactivity, such as sprays to condense steam and iodine, pumps and filters to remove radioactive dust, as well as cool walls to capture radioactive substances.

Isolation

The last defence is to site the reactor a long way from any large centre of population. Then, if all else fails and some of its radioactive contents spill over the countryside, the relatively few people in the danger zone can if necessary be safely evacuated, or other measures taken such as the temporary halting of local milk supplies, all in a manageable operation. The policy with early reactors—which is still followed for experimental ones—was to build them on very remote sites. With the growth of civil nuclear power and the consequent gain in experience however, together with the improvement of reactor safety and the increase in the numbers of reactors, the tendency has been to build nuclear power stations nearer the large centres of population, where the electricity is needed.

If the *very worst* were to happen—a complete melt-down and a total loss of containment—a power reactor could release something like 100 million curies of iodine−131 and 1 million curies of caesium−137 into the open air. With average wind conditions these could seriously contaminate a region of about 200 square miles, mainly in a narrow band extending some 20 to 30 miles downwind. If there were a large population in this region, and it were not quickly evacuated, there could be many people given doses likely eventually to cause cancer; and the level of radioactivity would remain unacceptably high for living there, for several years.

Policies on the siting of reactors rest on the degree of confidence that this ultimate accident cannot happen. For early Magnox reactors, the worst that could seriously be envisaged was a depressurisation with a melt-down and possibly burning in a single fuel channel. This would release about 10 to 100 curies of iodine, seriously affecting an area only some hundreds of yards beyond the site, and requiring the temporary stopping of milk from local farms up to about two miles downwind. These early reactors were required to be built not less than five miles from any town, and restrictions were also placed on the numbers of people living near them.

In the case of AGR a depressurisation is extremely unlikely; but even if it were to occur, the ensuing rise in temperature of the fuel would not reach anywhere near the melting point of either the can or the fuel. There is thus no credible way in which a melt-down could occur. Nevertheless a small amount of radioactivity might be released, about 10 curies, which would require a temporary ban on milk from farms one mile downwind. AGRs, because of their great public safety, are now allowed to be built quite close to urban areas.

Provided that the containment holds, the release from a water reactor or an LMFBR could again be no more than a few curies, which would affect only the immediate neighbourhood. Of course, a severe accident with a melt-down and badly breached containment could release a large amount of radioactivity over a region of several miles, highly dangerous to everyone in it. Such an accident is extremely unlikely but cannot be entirely ruled out.

The alarm at Harrisburg showed that more than public safety is at stake in the siting of nuclear reactors. Public *acceptability* is also required. This is harder to achieve than public safety, because it not only includes safety but also goes beyond it. For the general public, reactors not only have to *be safe*; they also have to be *seen to be safe*. One or two more accidents like that at Three Mile Island, coming fairly soon after one another in well-populated regions, and even with no casualties, would surely make nuclear power totally unacceptable to the general public. The isolation of nuclear plants in sparsely populated regions may thus be a necessary price that has to be paid for the long-term public acceptability of nuclear power [1].

References

1   Alvin Weinberg, *The Wilson Quarterly*, Summer Edition 1979, The Smithsonian Institution.

11

Margins of safety

Acceptable risks

It is easy to imagine a catastrophic reactor accident, with millions of curies suddenly spilled out over a built-up area and large numbers of casualties. But it is equally easy to point to the extremely safe record of civil nuclear energy, with no member of the public killed or injured through any accident from the large number of nuclear power plants now in use. What an extraordinary contrast this is! Two views of nuclear safety which are completely opposed! Yet each view contains elements which must be taken seriously. How are these two attitudes to be reconciled and unified into a single consistent viewpoint? This must be done if we are to find a rational approach to nuclear safety.

The answer can only come from taking into account the factor of *probability*. How likely is it that a given type of accident will occur? The big catastrophic accident is possible in principle, but extremely unlikely in practice. Indeed, even lesser but still bad accidents, in which small numbers of the general public would be harmed, are so improbable that none has happened so far.

On the other hand, of course, minor incidents which are easily rectified and harm no-one occur frequently, just as they do in any large and complex undertaking. And so we have to look at a whole range of possibilities, from the abundant but minor incidents at one extreme, right through to horrendous but almost impossible catastrophes at the other. A frequency of occurrence which is perfectly acceptable at the one extreme (although of course efforts are made to reduce it through good working practices) would become intolerable long before the other extreme is reached. What is therefore an *acceptable risk* varies enormously with the severity of the accident.

We thus have the double problem, not only of trying to judge what level of risk is publicly acceptable, but also of estimating how this level varies with the severity of the accident. How is this to be done? One starting point is to look at the frequencies of those accidents of varying severities in other fields of activity, which are accepted or at least tolerated by the general public. Bad fires occur from time to time in hotels, departmental stores and blocks of flats, in which numbers of people are killed. As a result, fire regulations may be tightened up, but people nevertheless do not abandon the use of such large buildings. They accept the risk. Similarly, air and rail transport are accepted by most people even though tragic crashes occur from time to time. There are other hazards, such as large petroleum and chemical stores situated in built-up areas, or carried by road or rail through them; and large dams which dominate inhabited valleys. Many accidents occur in which a few people are killed; from time to time there is one in which the number of fatalities runs to 100 or more; and occasionally, in some part of the world, there is a major catastrophe in which as many as 1,000 or more are killed. For example, while this chapter was being written (August 1980) 37 people were killed in a London fire, 69 in a Polish train accident, and 301 in an aircraft fire in Saudi Arabia—not forgetting more than 2,000 people killed some months previously, when the Gujarat Dam in India collapsed. Yet all these man-made hazards are allowed to continue—with constant insistence on higher safety standards of course—thereby demonstrating empirically what levels of risk are in the main tolerated by the public. And the public's tolerance of road casualties—in which the daily death toll amounts to several thousands in the year—seems to be limitless.

From the analysis of accident statistics it has been possible to put numbers to these various levels of risks. The most useful method is to express the likelihood of a given kind of accident in terms of its *frequency*—for example, the number per year of bad fires, or of air crashes—and to express its severity in terms of the *number of fatalities* it produces, within a given band of values[1]. For example, statistics in the USA show that on average a fire which kills between 30 and 300 people occurs about once in ten years; and this is expressed as an annual frequency of 0.1 for a fire in which the order of 100 people are killed. The results for all the various kinds of accidents are quite complex, of course, partly because the characteristics of fires, explosions, air crashes and dam failures all differ from one another, and partly because of scatter in the statistical data. But broad trends are nevertheless discernible; and these can be roughly summarised by saying that, for any one kind of accident, such as fires, or air crashes, the data lie not too far away from the relationship *frequency* × *number* = 10. For example, in a large industrial country, there occurs about 1 fire in a year in which the order of 10 people are killed; and 1 in 10 years in which the order of 100 are killed; and so on. In the case of accidents where the risk is less—for example the risk of a number of people on the ground being killed by an aircraft falling on them—the relationship is more like *frequency* × *number* = 1; e.g., the order of 10 people are killed by a single accident of this kind about once in 10 years.

These numbers, derived from real accidents of various kinds, indicate how much risk society actually tolerates in its various established activities. Would it be reasonable then to expect society to tolerate the lowest scale of these risks, i.e. *frequency* × *number* = 1, for nuclear power? In other words, if civil nuclear power killed people in the same numbers and frequencies as people are killed by aircraft falling on them, would this be publicly acceptable?

At this point we have to make a judgement. Even compared with aircraft, nuclear power is a new hazard and so cannot expect to enjoy that degree of acceptability which aircraft have now gained out of sheer familiarity, through people having 'learned to live with them'. Moreover, radiation is a silent, sinister, hazard and the harm it does—cancer —is particularly fearful. For these reasons, *frequency* × *number* = 1 is almost certainly too high a level of risk to be accepted for nuclear power. Some lower number is needed. What do we think would be acceptable? Would it be *frequency* × *number* = 0.0001 for *one* reactor? In a world of 1,000 such reactors, this means a total *frequency* × *number* = 0.1, i.e. one-tenth the risk of the same number of casualties hit on the ground by falling aircraft. A catastrophic nuclear accident which caused deaths of the order of 1,000 would occur, worldwide, once in about 10,000 years on this basis. Similarly, a single death, worldwide, might occur about once in ten years.

Would this be acceptable? We can only guess that it might, since it specifies a level of safety distinctly better than that of the least hazardous of the other man-made accidents mentioned above, and because it provides on average a large gap in time between casualties. If we regard this, then, as a *permitted* level of public risk for civil nuclear power, the next step is to express it in terms of the numbers of curies emitted. The estimates made by Farmer[1] based on iodine−131, which is likely to be the most harmful radioisotope emitted in a bad reactor accident, are necessarily uncertain because they depend on the direction and strength of the wind at the time of an accident, as well as on the siting of the reactor in relation to local populations; but for semi-urban sites they typically amount to 10 million curies for 1,000 casualties. This is about as much radiation as could reasonably be expected to escape and affect people, up to several miles away, in the worst type of reactor accident. On this basis, then, a *single* reactor should have a relationship *frequency* × *curies* = 1, or less. In other words, a single reactor should give a chance of less than once in ten million years of releasing ten million curies; or once in a thousand years of releasing one thousand curies; or once in a hundred years of releasing one hundred curies. This is the simplest version of the target suggested by Farmer for the margins of safety that might be accepted by the general public. Modifications to it have been suggested, to take account of the fact that people generally react more strongly to a single big accident than to a large number of little ones which, all together, cause the *same* total of casualties.

Keeping inside the target

Can reactors actually keep inside this target? In most branches of engineering such a question is usually answered by consulting the records of accidents and analysing them statistically; the numbers of bridges collapsed, boilers burst, aircraft crashed, how many people were killed in each case, and so on. Because the nuclear energy industry has so far been extremely safe, however, this method is not available. There have been no public casualties from nuclear accidents, and so no accident statistics. What has therefore had to be done, instead, is to *predict* the probabilities of reactor accidents by estimating the chances of various components going wrong, for which some statistics may be available, and then stringing together all these kinds of individual failures into possible sequences which lead to accidents of various types, sizes and likelihoods. This is the method that has been used by safety experts such as Farmer, as well as in the large US reactor safety study, WASH-1400, led by Rasmussen[1]. For a very simplified illustration of the kind of analysis used by Farmer[2] and Rasmussen, suppose that a large hole is formed in the pipework of a gas-cooled reactor, such that the gas pressure drops down towards atmospheric in about 5 minutes. This is of course an unlikely event. The safety systems which should then come into action automatically are, first, an immediate nuclear shut-down and second a switching on of gas blowers to keep the coolant circulating, using either normal or emergency power supplies. We have to work through the possibilities of various things going wrong with these safety systems, leading in each case to some outcome for the reactor. For each such outcome *two* numbers are required, one which gives the likelihood of the outcome occurring, the other which gives the amount of radioactivity likely to be released, especially the number of curies of iodine−131.

The worst possibility is that the shut-down system fails to work. In this case a bad accident is fairly certain and a sizeable fraction of the volatile radioactivity, of the order of 10 million curies, could escape. What is the chance of a shut-down failure? Experience shows that a single shut-down rod might fail to go in once in 10,000 demands. But a single failure does not stop shut-down. For this, several rods have to fail, and the chances of multiple failures are very much lower. For example, three rods of the above reliability, acting independently, are expected to fail simultaneously once in $10,000 \times 10,000 \times 10,000$, i.e. only once in a *million million* times of asking. Rasmussen in fact supposed that if three adjoining rods all failed, then the whole shut-down system had failed. Once in a million million times is exceedingly small, but in practice the risk might be higher than this because of the possibility of some common fault which causes all of them to fail. Such a possibility is itself very small but it might increase the risk to something like one in 1,000 million.

We have also to take into account the frequency of the pipework failure which starts off this accident sequence. Such an event has not occurred in practice and so must be much less than once a year. Nevertheless, Farmer assumed that a pipework failure accompanied by a shut-down failure could occur in a single reactor once in 100 million years. This is clearly far higher than the realistic frequency. Nevertheless, with 10 million curies released it falls well below the target limit of *frequency* × *curies* = 1.

If, when the pipework fails, the shut-down works successfully—as it is expected to do all but once in many hundreds of millions of times of asking—the next question is whether the blowers will fail. There are various possibilities here, which Farmer has shown how to estimate, taking into account the design of the cooling system and the known mechanical reliability of gas blowers and their power sources. The frequency with which all blowers might fail, on a single reactor, is estimated to be about once in a million years. This could release about 100,000 curies and so gives a relationship *frequency* × *curies* = 0.1, which is well inside the target. Partial failures of the blowers could also occur. The worst example here, in its combination of frequency and size of release, was estimated by Farmer to occur less than once in 10,000 years, per reactor, and to release about 1,000 curies. Again, this is well on the safe side of the required target.

Similar calculations have been made for water reactors by Rasmussen and Lewis[3]. A useful idea for all such work is the *event tree*. A highly simplified example for a loss-of-coolant accident in a water reactor is shown as follows:

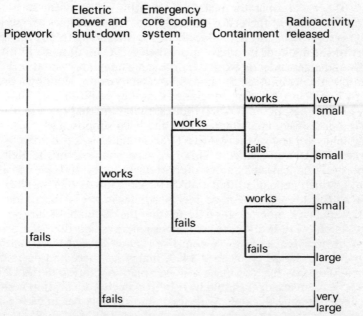

In this, starting from the initial event of a failure in the pipework, we can trace out various outcomes, ranging from the one extreme in which all the safety systems work satisfactorily to the other extreme in which they all fail. As an example we can, with only a minor adaptation, fit the Three Mile Island accident into this scheme. Leaving aside the earlier events in this accident, the first one which connects up with this event tree was the failure of the relief valve to close, thus providing the equivalent of a small failure in the pipework. Thereafter the shut-down *worked*, the ECCS *failed* (not mechanically but because it was manually throttled down), the containment building *worked* (substantially) and the radioactive release was *small*.

The value of analysis by event trees is that it compels one to look at all the possibilities and to give yes/no (i.e. works or fails) answers to each, so exposing all the various possible outcomes. When probabilities are calculated for the working or failing of each component, and then combined into a total probability for each outcome, with the likely radioactivity release also calculated for each case, then a *frequency* × *curies* figure can be given for each eventuality.

The reliability of safety analyses

How reliable are these methods? It is of course extremely difficult to estimate some of the individual probabilities, particularly when dealing with imaginary situations such as some hypothetical fault immobilising all the shut-down systems, or with the more likely possibility of a reactor operator mistakenly shutting off an essential valve or pump. Moreover, there are virtually no real examples of serious failures to provide any actual accident statistics. One test of the reliability of the methods is to have more than one team of analysts objectively and independently work over the same imaginary situations. For example, the Rasmussen Study has been analysed in detail by a group led by Lewis[4] in 1977, who concluded that they could find no bias, one way or the other, in the WASH-1400 estimates but that *uncertainties* in the estimates were much larger than had been supposed.

A single real test of the WASH-1400 estimates was provided by the Three Mile Island accident. This has been analysed in the Kemeny Report[5] (Technical staff analysis report on WASH-1400 reactor safety study), which concluded that 'WASH-1400 showed that small-break LOCAs (i.e. loss-of-coolant accidents) similar in size to the accident at TMI were much more likely to occur than the design basis large-break LOCAs, and can lead to the same consequences. Further, the probability of occurrence of an accident like that at Three Mile Island was high enough, based on WASH-1400, that since there had been more than 400 reactor years of nuclear power plant operation in the United States, such an accident should have been expected during that period.'

The dependence of safety analyses on the quality of engineering data is shown by the case of the steel pressure vessels used in light water reactors, which we discussed at the end of Chapter 9. In the Marshall Study (*loc. cit.*) the then accepted figure (about 95%) was taken for the probability of detecting a 1 inch crack by the best standard ultrasonic practice. This gives a probability of a pressure vessel failing—during an emergency or fault which temporarily reduces the critical crack size to 1 inch—which the Marshall Study estimated to be about 1 in 10,000. The estimated frequency of such an emergency or fault is about 1 in 1,000 years for a single reactor. Hence, with 10 million curies likely to be released by an accident in which the pressure vessel fails, the relationship *frequency* × *curies* = 1 is just satisfied with no margin to spare. However, as mentioned at the end of Chapter 9, recent tests of the reliability of ultrasonic inspections have shown that the chance of detecting a 1 inch crack is only about 50 percent. This gives a relationship *frequency* × *curies* = 10 which is *above* the limit of acceptability. That is why an improvement in crack inspection practice is needed, to raise the real reliability of crack detection up to at least the Marshall figure.

References

1 See F. R. Farmer, *Atom*, UKAEA, Number 230, December 1975; and N. C. Rasmussen, *Reactor Safety Study*, US Nuclear Regulatory Commission, *Report WASH-1400*, October 1975.
2 F. R. Farmer, *Atom*, UKAEA, Number 128, June 1967.
3 For an introductory account see H. W. Lewis, *Scientific American*, 242, 33, March 1980.
4 H. W. Lewis, *Risk Assessment Review Group Report to the US Nuclear Regulatory Commission*, National Technical Information Service, 1977.
5 J. G. Kemeny, *Report of the President's Commission on the accident at Three Mile Island*, Washington, October 1979.

12

To err is human

Paper, people and practice

It is the fate of the policy-maker to live in a paper world and to risk being deceived into thinking that it is the real one; into believing that to write is to act; that the written order, instruction or specification will of itself automatically bring about the intended real result; rather as, to the inhabitants of the paper world, the mere act of turning on a switch seems of itself to generate electricity. But between paper and practice stand *people*, the implementers who work with the real world in their hands and actually change it; people who in the nuclear industry weld up steel structures, fit and test valves and pumps, load and unload fuel rods, check the quality of materials and components, read instruments and press buttons in control rooms. Instead of the policy-maker's assumed automatic link which leads unswervingly from cause to effect, the instruction in reality is translated from paper to practice by the most flexible, unreliable, resourceful, unpredictable, interfering, imaginative and intelligent of links. The implementers cut corners, make mistakes, interpret unsatisfactory instructions intelligently and use their own initiatives in unexpected situations, sometimes making things worse by errors of judgement, sometimes brilliantly saving the day by original and effective actions.

Nuclear energy, of course, provides nothing new in all this. We all trust these same human qualities everyday in our ordinary lives. But they do stretch the problem of nuclear safety into another dimension, one of the utmost importance. This was brought out strongly in the Kemeny Report[1] on the accident at Three Mile Island, which said that: 'The equipment was sufficiently good that, except for human failures, the major accident at Three Mile Island would have been a minor incident. But, wherever we looked, we found problems with the human beings who operate the plant, with the management that runs the key organisation, and with the agency that is charged with assuring the safety of nuclear power plants.'

Human error has also played an important part in other serious reactor accidents. For example, in 1952 an operator's mistake led to the withdrawal of some control rods in a Canadian research reactor. The ensuing surge of nuclear reactivity then caused a partial melt-down and contaminated the reactor site with radioactivity. The Windscale fire in 1957 was triggered by an operator raising the power level too quickly in the mistaken belief, due to insufficient monitoring instruments, that the graphite temperature was everywhere too low for the Wigner energy release. And the fire at Brown's Ferry, Alabama, in 1975, which disabled many of the reactor's controls, was caused by an electrician's candle.

Reactor operators

The problems which face reactor operators in a sudden major crisis, and the mistakes which can be made by them on the spur of the moment, have been vividly described in the Kemeny Report's account of the accident at Three Mile Island. Up to 4.00 a.m. on 28 March 1979 everything was calm and normal, with no warning of the storm ahead. Five minutes later, all the primary events which set the reactor on course for a major accident had already happened. The pumps feeding water to the steam circuit stopped at 36 seconds after 4.00 a.m., thus beginning the whole incident. Then, in quick succession, the steam turbine switched itself off and the back-up feedwater pumps came on, exactly as required, but the operators failed to notice that the valves from these pumps were closed, no doubt because the warning lights for these were partly hidden by a maintenance tag in the control room. A pressure relief valve on the reactor coolant circuit had also opened correctly but then, a few seconds later, it failed to close. The operators were misled about this, because of a false indicator, and for a long time afterwards they acted on the assumption that the valve was closed, even though it was causing a loss-of-coolant accident which could have been avoided had they shut another blocking valve. The shut-down rods had already gone in automatically, as required, and the ECCS also switched on correctly at 2 minutes into the accident. But the operators, misled by signs of an apparent excess of water in the reactor, throttled the ECCS severely back at 4½ minutes into the accident. All these events were accompanied by an unhelpful cacophony of about 100 alarms sounding off, distracting the operators as they faced panel upon panel of red, green and amber lights, and dials indicating entirely unexpected combinations of conditions, and as they tried to grasp the significance of the mystifying changes that were happening to their reactor.

It is easy to criticise the operators' mistakes in handling this crisis. It is less easy to imagine oneself in the same position, having to perceive instantly the right thing to do when faced suddenly with a totally strange combination of events, and having to decide, out of all the many and confusing pieces of information that were flashing on the control panels, which were to be taken seriously and which ignored.

In view of all this, it is not surprising that the Kemeny Report was severely critical of the arrangements for controlling the reactor. The operators were inadequately trained for the task of handling an accident in which unusual combinations of events were occurring. They were not well served by the reactor instruments with significant information for diagnosing the problem. And they were distracted by a mass of unimportant detail, as well as by various alarms and warning lights, in an inadequately designed control room. The report called for various changes to be made, including a much improved system for training, qualifying and licensing reactor operators; better instrumentation and control room arrangements to help operators prevent accidents and to cope with them when they occur; and more complete training especially with *simulators* to prepare operators for a wide variety of accidents.

It is worth noting that in Britain the operators are required to be graduates, or the equivalent, and to be trained in understanding the plant and diagnosing conditions in it.

Responsibility

It has been said that the Three Mile Island accident was a blessing in disguise; that without physically harming anyone, it showed to the nuclear authorities how far in practice—as distinct from on paper—their actual reactor operating and emergency procedures fell below what was necessary. The British nuclear authorities had learned a similar lesson in 1957 from their Windscale reactor fire, after which they extensively revised their organisational arrangements and lines of responsibility.

In Britain the owners and operators of the civil nuclear power plants, i.e. the Electricity Generating Boards, are legally responsible for ensuring that no injuries to people or damage to property occur as a result of their activities. This was laid down in the Nuclear Installations Act and confirmed in the more recent Health and Safety at Work Act, which places full responsibility on employers for ensuring that no harm comes to anyone through their actions. Immediate responsibility for safety rests with the manager of each nuclear station and his staff, although he has the back-up support of many organisations. The generating boards themselves have nuclear health and safety staffs to ensure that proper safety provisions are made in the design, construction and operation of the nuclear stations; and at each station there are inspectors from these staffs to monitor the safety of the day-to-day operations. There is also a research and advisory service provided by the UKAEA's Safety and Reliability Directorate. Above all are the Nuclear Installations Inspectorate (NII), part of the government's independent Health and Safety Executive. The task of the NII is to assure themselves of the safety of nuclear plants and their operations, without which licences to operate cannot be issued. They work by regarding each plant as an individual special case, which has to be examined and assessed rigorously and in detail before it can be licenced to operate. In addition, emergency plans have to be provided, which are open to public inspection, for dealing with public emergencies and for informing the general public.

When it said in its report that 'the fundamental problems are people-related problems and not equipment problems' the Kemeny Commission emphasised that it meant by this, not just the shortcomings of individual human beings, but more general problems of the human organisations that make, run and control nuclear power plants. The Kemeny Commission noted a 'preoccupation with regulations'. The US Nuclear Regulatory Commission (NRC)—which has responsibility both for issuing operating licences for nuclear plants and for inspecting and enforcing safety regulations at these plants—had in the opinion of the Kemeny Commission concentrated too much on licensing, and had unduly relegated the second part of its responsibility to large books of complex regulations, which it required plant operators to obey and nuclear inspectors to monitor. In practice this reduced the industry's *direct* responsibility for safety by requiring it, instead, to concern itself with satisfying the regulations set down on paper.

The Kemeny Report has recommended widespread changes to rectify this situation, including an extensive reorganisation of the NRC. The general effect of these changes would be to bring the American practice much closer to the British, as outlined above. The intention in both countries now is to make the licenced reactor operator more directly responsible for the safety of the plant. The Kemeny Commission also criticised the somewhat fragmented character of the US electric supply industry, which consists of many independent companies, some of which are individually too small to be able to possess the necessary exceptional qualities of management and technical expertise for administering nuclear power plant up to the required standards. It thus recommended that companies must reach higher standards of organisation and management before they are given licences to operate nuclear power plant. In Britain this problem is eased by the integrated structures of the large electricity generating boards, which provide open channels for the flow of talent and experience between all stations and central staffs.

Human problems of automation

All the above takes us so far, but leaves some fundamental human problems about the running of reactors unresolved. First is the question of *automation*. How much of a station's safety system ought to be operated automatically, directly by signals received from the monitoring instruments, and how much should be left to the command of the operators? Under what circumstances should operators be enabled to over-ride the automatic control and safety systems and take *full* charge themselves? If a station is highly automated, what then is the *role* of the operators; and how can the complete automation of the vital safety features be reconciled with the need to have highly trained and extremely intelligent people in the control room? What is to be done about the *boredom* of such people, during long hours of steady and uneventful running? These are of course not questions specific to the nuclear industry. They apply to many modern activities which use advanced technology—for example, to the control of aircraft carrying large numbers of passengers, or to the navigation of highly automated cargo ships, or to the management of a continuous chemical production plant —and they are getting more difficult to answer as automatic control systems become more reliable and computers make them more versatile.

There must of course be a completely automatic system for bringing the major safety systems (emergency shut-down, back-up power, emergency cooling) into action immediately, directly upon command from the reactor's monitoring instruments. The automatic system must also be capable of dealing fully and satisfactorily with any *sudden* emergency. Human operators should not be required to take decisions which might affect public safety without first having time to reflect and consult. But what about all the other possibilities, the incidents which start off in a small way with minor failures—a stuck valve here plus a wrong instrument there—and which can evolve through a multitude of different possible courses? Can all of these be handled by a purely automatic system? The answer today, with large computers and advanced programmes, is probably *yes*. After all, even modest computers can now be programmed to play good games of chess, in which they are presented with the similar problem of working always towards a given end-point (victory for the chess-player, safety for the reactor controller), by providing the best calculated response to every conceivable and threatening move. The development of computer programmes, based on extensive research with reactor simulators to explore all kinds of sequences of 'moves', could provide the basis for this.

In these circumstances, what would the human reactor operators be expected to do? Could they be dispensed with entirely, and power stations be totally automatic? Would this gain any public confidence? Almost certainly not. We already have an example in civil aircraft, which can be flown on 'automatic pilot', guided by ground-based radio or radar signals, and landed 'blind' by modern equipment. Yet few of us would trust ourselves to a plane that lacked a human pilot. Why is this? Is it the feeling that, when all else goes wrong, we want to turn to human originality and resourcefulness in the hope of escaping the impending disaster? Indeed, these qualities have already proved themselves in nuclear accidents. Although human error has contributed a lot to some of these accidents, nevertheless at the same time human ingenuity has proved itself invaluable in successfully handling the ensuing crises and limiting the consequences of the accidents.

Even in highly automated control rooms, then, operators have to be present to oversee the functioning of the automatic systems and to be ready, in certain emergency conditions, to switch to manual control and really operate the reactor themselves. Clearly, the circumstances under which this intervention of the human operators takes place, and what they are allowed to do then, have to be very carefully worked out and clearly understood. And, since a complete technical understanding of the workings of the reactor would be essential for anyone who was licenced to override the automatic controls in an emergency, the operators have to be highly intelligent and highly trained.

How then are they to survive the boredom of the long stretches of routine running without losing their effectiveness? What many intelligent people do, when called upon to endure a long inactive period such as a train journey, is to solve crossword puzzles or play chess. Simulated reactor incidents can, as we have seen, resemble games of chess. Should not the operators therefore, in addition to routine monitoring during their normal periods on duty, be required to practice handling reactor incidents on a simulator, for both intellectual exercise and operational training? The number of possible combinations of different minor faults is so large that such 'games' could be open-ended and almost inexhaustible in their variety.

References

1 J. G. Kemeny, *Report of the President's Commission on the accident at Three Mile Island*, Washington, October 1979.

13

Nuclear inheritance

A moral question

It has been said that we, in this present age, are acting immorally in producing from our civil nuclear programmes long-lived radioactive wastes, that will be a burden and hazard to future generations. Such moral feelings may seem out of place when we are, at the same time, greedily and recklessly using up limited natural resources such as oil, so stripping the cupboard bare for our successors; when we are also releasing long-lived radioactivity into the air and topsoil by burning coal and excavating earth in large amounts; and are spreading poisons such as arsenical herbicides over our farmlands in much more toxic amounts than the radioactive products released from our nuclear programmes.

But what really matters is not why some people are so particularly sensitive to the issue of nuclear waste, but whether there is substance in their charge that we shall be burdening future generations with a serious radioactivity hazard.

The natural world beneath our feet contains thousands of millions of tons of uranium. This has an extremely long half-life (4,500 million years) and, as it slowly decays into radium, radon, etc., it and they expose us—and everything and everyone for millions of years to come—to that most damaging form of radiation, alpha particles. All this is part of the natural burden of life itself on this terrestrial planet. There has been a recent change, however, which will make the future different from the past. Through the discoveries of nuclear physics we have found a way, not only of tapping a new source of energy, but also of making a change, albeit a minute one, in the distribution and character of this inevitable radioactivity. We now take extremely small amounts from the earth's stock of uranium and, in nuclear reactors, make these disintegrate much more quickly. As a result, for each uranium atom which disappears through fission, a few new radioactive atoms mainly of the beta and gamma emitting kind appear. Most of these new atoms quickly disintegrate inside the reactor, and about 90 percent of the remainder also do so during the sojourn of the fuel rods in the cooling ponds, after their removal from the reactor.

The net *long-term* result, therefore, of man's nuclear activities is a *reduction* in the world's number of radioactive atoms. But what matters of course is not the number of atoms but their *radioactivity*, which depends on half-lives as well as numbers. Even here, if we take a sufficiently long view, the result of man's efforts is to *reduce* the world's radioactivity slightly, because we are consuming some uranium atoms and replacing them with radioactive products which mostly have short half-lives and so quickly decay into inactive species. Admittedly, we are making only insignificant long-term changes, but that is because human nuclear efforts are so minute compared with the earth's.

On a really long time-scale, then, there is no moral case against us. The charge, if it has validity at all, is not one for the very far future but for the next few hundred years, when some of the radioactive products of today's programmes will still be quite active.

The long-term decrease in the earth's radioactivity, due to our efforts, is gained at the expense of a short-term increase. It is as if we were somehow able, through our nuclear programmes, to 'squeeze up' the 4,500 million year half-life of some of the earth's uranium atoms into periods of seconds, hours, days and a few years. This is not to be taken literally of course, since the natural decay of a uranium nucleus, through alpha particle emission, is quite different from disintegration by fission. But it does give an idea of the sweeping up of a more or less fixed amount of radioactivity, back from astonomically long times into times on a human scale, as a result of our intervention in the earth's nuclear processes.

From 4,500 million years down to seconds, days, even centuries, is a tremendous squeezing up of the timescale. Not surprisingly, then, the radioactivity of nuclear fuel rods, freshly withdrawn from an active reactor, is some million times greater than that of the natural uranium ore from which they were made. But this radioactivity, just because it is so very intense, dies away quickly at first and then more gradually, eventually becoming weaker than the natural radioactivity of the ore. After the first year (e.g. in the cooling ponds) it is still about 10,000 times as active as the ore, weight for weight. After most of the uranium and plutonium have then been removed in the reprocessing plant, the remaining radioactive waste drops in 10 years to about 1,000 times the activity of the ore, and after about 1,000 years it drops right down to the same activity as the ore. Thus, after this time has elapsed, the radioactive waste is no more harmful than the natural earth from which its parent fuel was made. The important problems of the nuclear inheritance are, for this reason, to be sought in the first several hundred years.

Highly active wastes

As we saw in Chapter 6, after reprocessing, most of the radioactive waste from a power reactor is stored in highly concentrated acid solutions in safe vessels. Double stainless steel tanks are used for this purpose, and the space between their walls is monitored for leakage from the inner tank. Pumps are also provided to remove any such leaked fluid to another tank. The fluids are cooled by water pipes passing down into them, which remove the approximately 2,000 kilowatts of heat generated by the thousands of millions of curies of radioactivity in each fully loaded tank. The security of the water cooling is ensured by multiple back-up pumps, but if it were to fail the solution would not boil dry for some days and even then virtually all the radioactive substances would remain in the tank.

The need for cooling drops away in time, as the radioactivity gradually decays. After ten years the short-lived isotopes which produce most of the heat are largely gone but there still remains around 100 million curies in a tank. It would be entirely feasible to leave the solutions to continue decaying radioactively, gradually over several centuries, until they had become sufficiently inert to be capable of being poured away in a diluted form. This would not be difficult technically, especially as the *volume* of highly active liquid is very small. For example, practically all the waste from the entire 25-year British nuclear programme is contained in ten tanks at Windscale, each the size of a small room. However, when planning centuries ahead it is not good enough simply to rely on a system which demands, for its safety, the continuing care and maintenance by future generations. A form of disposal is needed which will remain safe without such care.

Fortunately, the smallness of the volume of highly active wastes makes this possible. Even if *all* electricity were produced from nuclear energy, one person's entire nuclear wastes for a year's electricity could be reduced to the size of one cigarette. Because of this smallness, quite exceptionally elaborate processes and high standards of containment and isolation could be afforded. The first step in these would be to convert the wastes, after ten years or so in the tanks, into a stable *solid* form in which they are no longer able to spill, leak, spread or vaporise. The virtues of solids for the safe holding of things over long times are obvious. Fossil insects, many millions of years old, have been found perfectly preserved in amber. Mammoths have emerged from glaciers after 30,000 years, with their meat still fresh and edible. Egyptian pyramids have stood the test of time; and ancient decorated glassware, 3,500 years old, remains in perfect condition today with no significant deterioration or erosion of the glass or running of the colours.

Glass in fact is the proposed material for the solidification of nuclear wastes, which combine well with the standard ingredients used in glassmaking. They can then be rendered into very stable glasses, similar to pyrex, containing about 15 per cent of fission products and with good resistance to heat, chemical action, radiation and mechanical stress. Even in flowing warm water (at 40°C) it takes a century to dissolve away about 1 millimetre off the surface of such a glass.

The general plan is to cast these nuclear-containing glasses into solid columns, each about the height of a room and the diameter of a barrel. A year's waste from one 1,000 megawatt (electrical) nuclear station could be contained in seven of these. Each glass cylinder would be sealed in a stainless alloy container, chosen to resist corrosion for thousands of years in a dry environment. In case it might become exposed to corrosive natural waters, this container would be covered with an outer layer of some other corrosion-resistant substance such as copper or lead—which is known from archaeology to be able to resist salt water for more than 1,000 years.

The *heat* of radioactivity has to be removed from these containers. Initially this is about 10 kilowatts from each. This is too much merely to be conducted away naturally, through rocks, without subjecting them to severe high temperature stresses. For the first 30 to 50 years, then, the containers would be stored in water ponds or air cooling chambers, probably at the reprocessing plant. After this time, the heat output will have declined sufficiently to allow the containers to be transferred to boreholes in rocks, where natural cooling is adequate. They can then remain permanently immured in deep vaults, about half-a-mile below ground. The access tunnels to these vaults would eventually be filled in with rocks and earth. The advantage of going to such depths is that in inactive parts of the earth's crust, the geological structures and materials down there remain stable for millions of years. The only major geological event which might occur in the nearer future is another ice age. But the experience of past ice ages, during the last 10,000 to one million years, shows that the glaciers do not on average scrape away the surface of the land to a depth beyond about one-quarter of a mile (and in so doing, by grinding up granite and releasing its natural uranium content, they deliver to the open environment much larger amounts of radioactivity than could come from the vaults).

The preferred places for the burial of the cylinders—a few thousand in each vault, spaced out to allow each to be separately cooled by its surrounding material—are in geologically dry deposits of granite, in thick salt beds or in clay-rich rocks. Granite rock is generally impervious to water, as well as being extremely stable geologically. Salt, and also to some extent clay, has the advantage that cracks in it seal themselves up by plastic flow. Clay has the further advantage of being attractive to many atoms, and so would tend to hold on to any radioactive atoms which happened to escape from their containers.

The safety of natural stores

What are the possibilities of such escapes and how dangerous could they be? The main danger is that the radioactive substances might by some means get dissolved in water, which would eventually find its way to the surface, or into wells as drinking water. For this to happen, several distinct barriers would have to be breached. First, the geological nature of the region would have to change from dry to wet, and the rocks surrounding the containers would have to become penetrated by the water, in order for this both to reach the containers and afterwards percolate to the surface. Then the corrosion-resistant envelopes would have to be penetrated, to expose the glass to the water. Next, the glass itself would have to be attacked by the water sufficiently to release significant amounts of its radioactive materials. These would need to dissolve in the water and then be swept along with it, despite the numerous opportunities for their deposition on all the mineral surfaces which the outgoing water would meet on its long journey to the surface. And in making its journey, this water would not have to become unduly diluted by confluence with other, uncontaminated, streams.

Plain commonsense shows that the chance of any substances in the glass getting past all these barriers, in significant amounts, and in time still to be seriously radioactive when they finally emerge in drinking water, must be extraordinarily small. Calculations have in fact been made of the radioactive hazard which might result from such escapes. Even though based on very pessimistic assumptions, these calculations show that the hazard is extremely small. For example, the National Radiological Protection Board[1] estimated that even in the worst case, no-one would receive a dose of more than a few percent of the ICRP dose limit. Similarly, a Swedish study[2] showed that in the most unfavourable case—i.e. a deep drinking-water well drilled close to the nuclear deposit—this would increase the annual personal radiation dose to someone using the well regularly by not more than 0.013 rem, which is well below the *variations* in natural radiation between different places of abode. It was pointed out, moreover, that even these estimates were based on assumed rates of dissolution of the containers and the glass far higher than were ever likely to apply in practice. American studies[3] have likewise shown that it would take hundreds of thousands of years for radioactive substances to escape from their containers to the surface, by which time their activity would be very low. Underground sites do not change their geological nature, e.g. from dry to wet, except over times running into millions of years. But even if water did reach a salt deposit, the dissolution of this would take thousands of years. After another long period in getting through the corrosion-resistant containers, the water might then begin to leach the glass at a rate of about 1 percent a century. Underground water typically takes about 1,000 years to reach the surface from the depths at which the wastes would be buried, but the radioactive materials would travel 100 to 10,000 times slower than this because they would be continually trapped on the surfaces of the minerals through which the water was percolating. Useful summaries of these various studies have been given by Roberts and Cohen[4].

There still remains the possibility that nuclear escapes could be brought about by human action, either deliberately by terrorists or accidentally by mining engineers. As regards the first, the setting up of a major and long-term mining operation, by digging a tunnel through a mile or so of rock to get at large heavy slabs of glass, which then have to be removed and finally specially treated to release their radio-activity, hardly seems a credible basis for a terrorist operation. There are easier ways of committing an outrage. As regards more extreme possibilities, even an atomic bomb exploded on the surface would not break up the deeply buried material beneath.

The problem of accidentally mining the deposits cannot exist so long as there is a continuity of organised society; but in any case the sites being considered for nuclear waste are deliberately selected for their unattractiveness as sources of minerals. Even if salt deposits were used, the chance of one of these being accidentally chosen for mining, from among all the great numbers available, is very small. Merely striking the containers with mining machinery would not, of course, release more than a trace of radioactivity. For a large release, the glass would have to be finely ground up or vapourised, at or near the surface, which could not happen accidentally.

Down to earth

The glass cylinders, their containers, the impermeable rock round them, and the dryness of the site, provide extremely good barriers to the release of radioactive waste. But suppose that by some malevolent miracle they became completely ineffective; that the waste became as freely and openly distributed, underground, as natural radioactive substances. How much could become a hazard then? This has been examined[3] by comparing the amounts of radium contained naturally in the top layers of the earth's surface with known small amounts which find their way into the human body. The conclusion is that the surfaced waste from one year's operation of all-nuclear power in the USA would produce one fatality per 2½ million years. The basic point is that, although the waste is highly concentrated, its amount is minute compared with the natural radioactive content of the surface layers of the earth. On average, then, through ordinary natural processes, the amount of released man-made radioactivity brought up to the surface would similarly be extremely small compared with the amount of natural radioactivity brought up. The point has been put vividly by Hoyle[5], thus: 'The hills of the English Lake District generate within themselves as much radioactive energy as would come from the buried waste products of three or four large nuclear power plants. This natural radioactivity, lying above sea level, inevitably has the heavy rains of the Lake District percolating through it, not water that is imag-ined to rise miraculously upward from great depth. Yet experience shows that the natural radioactivity of the Lakeland hills does *not* wash out in our streams and rivers'.

There is also a more direct example. The world's first nuclear reactor existed without any containment whatsoever and was allowed to spill its contents freely into the surrounding rocks, waters and soil. All this happened 1,800 million years ago, at Oklo in west equatorial Africa, where a chance arrangement of rich uranium deposits and ground-water moderator produced conditions favourable for the formation of a *natural* light-water reactor[6]. This performed for nearly a million years, generated about 15,000 megawatt-years of energy, which is comparable with the lifetime output of a medium-sized nuclear power station, released several tons of fission products as well as some plutonium, and was discovered by geologists in 1972 from evidence of anomalies in the distribution of isotopes in the local uranium deposits. Scientifically, of course, the Oklo reactor is a fascinating phenomenon. But from our present point of view, its main interest lies in the fact that the fossil traces of this ancient reactor, i.e. its fission products and actinide elements, have remained closely localised to the original site, despite exposure to water and geological processes over a period spanning almost half of the earth's whole time of existence.

In fact, if we really want to worry about releases of radioactivity from the earth, we should concern ourselves much more with emissions of radon-creating uranium from coal-fired power stations and from large earth-moving operations, for these present radioactive hazards to future generations which, although extremely minute, are nevertheless larger than those from deep underground nuclear waste deposits.

The Swedish study, mentioned above[2], concluded with the words: 'The proposed method for the final storage of high-level waste glass is therefore deemed to be absolutely safe'. Except in the most narrowly pedantic sense, the word 'absolutely' is surely fully justified in this case.

References

1   M. D. Hill and P. D. Grimwood, *Report NRPB-R69*, National Radiological Protection Board, January 1978;

2   *Karn-Bransle-Sakerhet Report*, AB Teleplan, Solna, Sweden, 1978.

3   B. L. Cohen, *Reviews of Modern Physics*, 49, 1, January 1977.

4   L. E. J. Roberts, *Atom*, 267, 8, January 1979, UKAEA; B. L. Cohen, *Scientific American*, 236, 21, June 1977.

5   Fred Hoyle, *Energy or Extinction?*, Heinemann Educational, London, 1977.

6   See, for example, R. Naudet, *Interdisciplinary Science Reviews*, 1, 72, 1976.

14

Security

Nuclear terrorism

We live in a violent age. It is perhaps the most violent since that of the great religious wars, which it somewhat resembles in the degree of support given to the fanatic's doctrine that ends justify means. Embassies are stormed, innocent hostages taken, protesting crowds shot down, buildings bombed, petroleum plants burnt, trains wrecked and airliners hi-jacked. Political murder has become an overt governmental practice in some countries. The violent forces in human nature, at best hardly restrained by the delicate gauze of civilisation, have been inflamed by extremists; and ideology has sanctified barbarism.

Is this a world safe for nuclear energy? Are civil nuclear plants especially vulnerable to terrorist actions? Do they offer terrorists particularly tempting opportunities to hold society to ransom? Over and above other sensitive industrial targets they have two features which give them unique importance. First, they produce radioactive substances. It is conceivable that terrorists might get hold of these and release them, or threaten to do so, among the general population. Second, nuclear plants produce and work with substances that are potential nuclear explosives. There is thus the possibility that terrorists might try to steal plutonium, for example, and make an atomic bomb.

The possibility of releasing radioactive substances depends on the ability of terrorists to get hold of large amounts, and on their having a preference for this method of attacking society rather than any other. The very fact that the general public has such a great fear of atomic radiation would no doubt be, for some terrorist groups, a point in favour of this method. But in most other respects, the arguments go against it.

This is because radioactive substances are hard to acquire by irregular means and in large amounts, and because they are very difficult and dangerous to handle. The various safety systems built into all nuclear plants (for the reasons discussed in previous chapters) also provide a measure of *security* against human actions. The barriers which prevent radiation getting from the plant to the public outside, also serve to some extent as barriers against outsiders getting to the plant inside. There are three main security systems for a major nuclear plant: first, the distant outer fence round the site, together with the gateway staffs at the entrance; second, the strong containment buildings and massive concrete shielding in which the key parts of the plant are enclosed; third, the special protective measures for the main safety systems, such as automatic operation, multiple and independent back-up systems, and strict procedures for authorising the entry of people into the control rooms and other key areas.

The outer boundary could of course be penetrated, although it would generally require a group of determined and armed people to force their way in. Power supplies to the site might be cut off, but emergency stand-by supplies inside the site are already provided for other reasons. The massive concrete shielding could not be more than superficially damaged by small bombs, and the containment buildings are deliberately intended to withstand minor blasts. It would be difficult for a group of intruders to force their way into the control room. If they did succeed in this, the security of the plant would then depend upon the shut-down and emergency safety systems coming automatically into operation as soon as a significant irregularity—whether due to a malfunction of the plant itself, or a dangerous instruction from the control room—made itself known; and upon these systems then remaining in operation until confirmatory signals for their release were received from an independent command centre outside the site. The principle for this kind of security is not basically different from that of control room safety in the event of a natural accident, i.e. that the complete system of emergency safety devices (with back-up alternatives) should work automatically, and that the people in the control room should also be able to bring these devices into action, but should not by themselves, without external and independent confirmatory signals, be able to take them out of action.

Smaller terrorist efforts might be attempted against more limited targets; for example a bazooka attack on a transporter container carrying spent fuel rods through a built-up area. As an exercise in terror, such an attack would not make much sense. Heavy weapons would be needed to penetrate the thick steel casing; and the results, although serious in the immediate locality of a breached container (so that the terrorists themselves would be in the first line of casualties), would be on a small scale. It would not be an attractive target for either ease of attack or spectacular consequences.

Terrorists might try to steal some highly radioactive material which is in transit and then release it, or threaten to do so, in a densely populated place. For example, they could put it in the ventilation system of a big building. Such an action would be fraught with difficulty, including the technical one that most of the radioactive substances transported in large amounts on public routes are not readily vaporisable, and are generally embodied in solid material. Quite apart from the problems of getting hold of such substances and of handling them without becoming exposed to their radioactive effects, there is the special difficulty—as compared with, say, chemical poison gases or volatile sprays of dangerous pathogens—of releasing such substances in a sufficiently fine form to float in the air. Speculations about these possibilities usually focus on *plutonium* as the substance which terrorists might try to spread about. Certainly, if inhaled as fine dust into the lungs it is very dangerous; but getting it into this state and spreading it widely would be both difficult and extremely hazardous for the perpetrators.

'Home-made' atomic bombs

Nuclear power stations make use of the fissioning of certain nuclei. So do atomic bombs. It is thus hardly surprising that many people fear that the two are inextricably linked; that the very existence of a civil nuclear power programme is bound, by one means or another, to lead to the further spread of nuclear weapons throughout the world, perhaps even to such an extent that quite small terrorist groups might become able to make crude bombs.

In theory it is simple to make an atomic explosion. Place together two or more small pieces of either uranium-235 (or uranium-233) or plutonium, so as to form a total lump of about the size of a grapefruit and hold them there long enough for fission to spread widely among their atoms. The energy which this releases can match that of many thousands of tons of dynamite. Uranium-235 or plutonium are suitable because their nuclei are fissioned by fast (i.e. unmoderated) neutrons; and so, if a sufficiently large number of these nuclei are brought together in a *super-critical assembly*, the process can be spread contagiously from one nucleus to another by promptly released neutrons.

In practice it is very hard to make an atomic bomb. Quite apart from the difficulty of obtaining undiluted nuclear explosive material— reactor fuel is quite useless in this respect because it contains a lot of neutron-absorbing uranium-238 nuclei—there are immense problems in the safe handling of these extremely hazardous materials and in the construction of the bomb itself. The size and arrangement of the small pieces, as well as those of the assembled bomb, have to be calculated carefully in order both to avoid criticality *before*, and to achieve super-criticality *after*, they are assembled. A most important condition for a large explosion is that the pieces have to be brought together exceptionally quickly and then held there long enough to get extensive fissioning before the nuclei and neutrons are eventually driven apart, out of one another's reach, by the force of the explosion. If the pieces are brought together only at more ordinary speeds, e.g. at the speed of a hand-clap, the nuclear reaction would begin long before they were fully assembled and they would start to fly apart again before more than a few of their nuclei had reacted. This would produce a *criticality incident* (see Chapter 8), with a puff of energy and a local release of radiation, rather than a full nuclear explosion. While the very advanced techniques used for producing large explosions are almost certainly beyond the scope of 'amateur' bomb-making teams, simpler methods could undoubtedly be devised, within the scope of a skilled and determined team in possession of good workshop facilities and plenty of lead shielding, that could deliver an atomic explosion with the force of several tons of dynamite. The general scale of the difficulty should not however be underestimated. Even where an entire country has decided to become a nuclear weapon power, and has been able to enlist its national technical, industrial and financial resources in the project, it has generally had to spend a few years on making and testing its first bomb. The mildest 'amateur' bomb would take a large number of highly skilled and well-equipped people many months to construct, during which time they would, without the elaborate protective facilities that only a national effort could provide, be exposed to considerable personal danger.

Sources of nuclear explosive

The 'amateur' bomb-makers would not only have to solve the above problems. They would also have to get hold of nuclear explosive. This is the point at which there could, in principle, be a link between civil nuclear energy and nuclear terrorism, because nuclear reactors produce *plutonium*.

There are two main ways to make nuclear explosives: to use *isotope separators* to extract uranium−235 from natural uranium; or to use *nuclear reactors* and *reprocessing plants* to make and extract plutonium from uranium.

First, isotope separation plants: these are of course also used in civil nuclear energy to produce *enriched nuclear fuel* for several kinds of reactors; but the degree of separation required for this is far below that necessary to produce the nearly pure uranium−235 suitable for a nuclear explosive. Except for this, there is no link between civil nuclear energy and *uranium* bombs, as is shown by the fact that the building of separation plants and the production of such bombs has usually occurred independently of the development of civil nuclear industries. It is in fact perfectly possible to set up a bomb-making capability in a country where there is no civil nuclear programme.

Several methods are now known for the separation of uranium isotopes. The two main ones are by *gaseous diffusion* and by *centrifuging*, but there are others, such as *electromagnetic separation* or the use of *aerodynamic jets* or *laser beams*. Some of them require enormous industrial resources. All are slow, expensive and involve advanced science and engineering.

For these reasons, *plutonium* might be thought a more attractive explosive than uranium−235, for an 'amateur' group. But it also sets many problems. As we shall discuss in the next chapter, plutonium is produced in a highly inaccessible form, with two formidable barriers to be overcome before it can be used as a nuclear explosive: the *radiation* barrier of the intensely active fuel rods in which it is dispersed; and the *chemical* barrier of the difficult processes necessary for separating it from the uranium and fission products, in these fuel rods, at a reprocessing plant.

There are also other problems due to the fact that, in a reactor, not only is plutonium−239 produced, which is the isotope suitable for nuclear explosive, but also plutonium−240. This second isotope undergoes fission spontaneously, releasing neutrons. If there is much of it in the bomb material, the neutrons then flying about could set off the chain reaction prematurely while the pieces are still being brought together and the explosion would thus be a minor one. As a result, the simpler methods of bringing the pieces together—such as firing two hemispheres together in a gun—are rather ineffective for plutonium. Only the most advanced methods (*implosion*) can produce large explosions. For this reason, plutonium is a more difficult 'amateur' bomb material than uranium−235.

The other point about plutonium−240 is that the longer a fuel rod remains in a reactor, the more the plutonium consists of this isotope. This is why there is generally a difference between military production and civil power reactors. In a military production reactor the fuel rods are inserted for relatively brief periods, so as to minimise the amount of the 240 isotope in the plutonium. Although dual-purpose reactors are possible, the usual aim in civil reactors is quite the opposite of this. It is to keep the fuel rods in for long periods so as to extract really large amounts of power from them. This produces a higher content of 240, so that this plutonium is much less suitable for bomb-making. In addition to this basic divergence between the technologies for military and civil purposes, there is also of course the fact that a military production reactor can be much simpler than a civil power one, because it does not need all the elaboration associated with the high temperatures and pressures of power reactors.

The link between civil nuclear energy and the spread of nuclear weapons is thus less direct than might at first sight be supposed. We shall look at it again in the next chapter. The problems for terrorists in trying to obtain material from civil nuclear plant, convert it into a bomb, and then set this off effectively, are clearly quite formidable. Stealing irradiated fuel elements would not take them very far along this road and would put their own lives in great danger. Obviously they could by-pass many of these problems by stealing, not the raw material, but the processed explosive, or even a finished bomb. The tight security which protects the large number of atomic bombs now in existence has clearly been effective. The security protecting nuclear materials or even processed explosive would have to be very much inferior to this before it became advantageous for a terrorist group to aim at stealing these, with all the problems to be faced thereafter, rather than stealing a complete atomic bomb.

The threat to civil liberties

It is sometimes said that the security system needed to protect nuclear materials from being stolen, especially plutonium, may itself become a threat to civil liberties; that it could lead to a kind of police state, with heavily armed security guards making their presence felt oppressively on people generally. This objection can hardly be taken seriously. All countries already have military forces which are far larger than the security forces needed to protect civil nuclear plant. Few of us feel oppressed or our civil liberties threatened when we happen to meet a military vehicle on a road, or drive past the fence of a defence establishment, or meet a few soldiers in the high street.

There are also large numbers of security people employed in delivering money, guarding government buildings and industrial establishments, etc., and most of us do not feel noticeably oppressed by them. Airport security is also now very strict. While we may occasionally feel irritated at the searches which are made of ourselves and our luggage, when we go to board an aircraft, we do not usually feel oppressed by this and are, at heart, mostly glad that our safety from terrorist action is being cared for in this way. The additional amount of security needed for protecting nuclear plants and materials, again for our safety, is very small compared with what we already have—and mostly find entirely acceptable—for all these other purposes.

15

Plutonium economy

The two roads

We are now approaching a crucial junction in civil nuclear power. If we take one road, continuing with the kind of thermal reactors we already have, then nuclear power will not last long. These reactors are too wasteful in their use of uranium; and ores of the richness necessary to feed them are scarce and likely to be all used up soon in the next century. The usefulness of thermal reactors might be prolonged by developing less wasteful types, for example based on the use of the heavy-water moderator (as in the Candu reactor) or on the use of thorium as a reactor material, but these improvements will need a lot of research and cannot be guaranteed to be successful at this stage.

The other road takes us to new types of reactor. It is possible that the *fusion* type may be successfully developed, to provide almost unlimited amounts of energy by the formation of helium nuclei from hydrogen isotopes. The most immediate possibility, however, is through breeder reactors, whereby the common uranium isotope–238 is converted into fissionable *plutonium*—a nuclear fuel. Along this road, later in the next century, there could be a few thousand power stations in the world, mostly of the *fast breeder reactor* (FBR) type, all running on plutonium fuel. To service these, some 50 to 100 reprocessing plants could be needed and over 30,000 tons of plutonium. If the reactors and reprocessing plants were to be mostly on different sites, there might have to be some 100,000 shipments of plutonium-based fuel a year.

All this busy activity would constitute the *plutonium economy*, about which the Flowers Report[1] so strikingly cautioned us. To quote from the report: 'Such proliferation of reactors, nuclear plants and shipments of nuclear materials throughout the world will certainly greatly increase the probability of accidents and the opportunities for malevolence ... ... with the present state of nuclear development and with the security measures that are now in force or are being introduced, the risks to society from illicit activities are small. The main concern lies with a future in which there could be substantial growth in nuclear power and a move into the plutonium economy'.

The main fear is that a busy and competitive international trade in civil plutonium fuel could open the way to the diversion of large amounts into the hands of terrorists and political extremists, for bomb-making. The other way in which terrorists could use plutonium—by releasing it or threatening to release it in the atmosphere—is much less practicable, for it would be very difficult to arrange this in a controlled and effective way (as has been shown in Chapter 14). In fact, as a by-product of the atmospheric atomic bomb tests of the 1950s and 1960s, some five tons of plutonium have already been released into the atmosphere around the world, with no medically detectable effects. The real problem of the plutonium economy is not atmospheric contamination, but the possible diversion of civil plutonium into bombs.

Fuel cycles

The annual plutonium output of a 1,000 megawatt (electrical) thermal reactor of the PWR type is a little over ¼ ton. The gross production is actually a good deal more than this, but about ⅔ of the plutonium made in the reactor is also consumed in the reactor, by fission. The remaining ¼ ton could not be used as a nuclear explosive as it stands, because it is dispersed thinly among many tons of uranium−238 in the fuel rods. When first taken out of the reactor, these rods are too fiercely radioactive to handle, even in a standard reprocessing plant; and they remain too active to handle in the ordinary way for many years. Only after they have gone through a reprocessing plant—where their plutonium is separated from its associated uranium and radio-active fission products—does this plutonium become a material that terrorist groups might be able to handle and make into bombs.

We see that one possible way to avoid this danger is simply *never to separate the plutonium from its fuel rods*. This is the principle of the 'once-through' or 'throw-away' fuel cycle, recently favoured by the USA authorities. The spent fuel rods from civil reactors are not reprocessed, but simply stored indefinitely in safe places, where their intense radioactivity protects their plutonium from theft. This pluton-ium is technically 'inaccessible' to all except very large governmental forces, primarily because it is enveloped in intense radiation, and secondarily because it is atomically dispersed amongst the uranium and fission products in the fuel rods.

However, there are two things wrong with this throw-away cycle. First, it wastes the plutonium as reactor fuel, and hence wastes the abundant uranium−238 which is the source of the plutonium. Fission nuclear power would soon die out, on this basis, through lack of fuel. Second, the radiation barrier, so formidable at first, gradually decays away over the years into something much less ferocious. The fuel rods become increasingly approachable and their plutonium is no longer inaccessible. These are slow changes, which depend on the gradual decay of the radioactivity in the fuel rods. But, as the Flowers Report emphasised, it is important in nuclear policy to look a long way ahead, so as to avoid 'solutions' that are satisfactory at first but leave difficult problems for future generations. The throw-away cycle is only a short-term solution. At best, it could buy some years of time while other and more permanent solutions are developed and afterwards applied to its temporarily stored fuel rods.

The alternative strategy is to reprocess the spent fuel rods soon after they leave their reactors, extract their plutonium, mix it with uranium−238, make it up into new fuel rods and then get these quickly back into the reactors. In this way, the plutonium is both used as fuel and also enveloped once more in intense radioactivity, so making it inaccessible again. This plutonium fuel *could* be used in thermal reactors—which might occur in the near future, so long as these continue to be the main type of reactor. However, for various reasons, it is in the long term much more likely to be used in fast breeder reactors. The main advantage of these is that, with the aid of repeated recycling, they can convert the majority of the uranium−238 isotope into plutonium and use it as fuel. From the security point of view they also have the advantage of being *consumers* of plutonium, as well as breeders, so that the *net* output of plutonium from an FBR is generally much less than that of a thermal reactor of the same electrical output.

Once the reprocessed plutonium is back in an active reactor it quickly becomes protected by radioactivity and so rendered inaccessible. The danger in this fuel cycle is thus limited to the period after the plutonium has been extracted and separated from its old fuel rods, but before it is back in a reactor in its new fuel rods. About a third of the total plutonium involved in the whole fuel cycle would be at this vulnerable stage. Various ways of reducing or eliminating this risk have now been proposed.

One of them is the *power park*—the idea of having reactors, reprocessing and fuel rod plants all on the same site, so that the plutonium from and for those reactors never has to go outside the site. This scheme will be tried at Dounreay, Scotland, where a fuel plant is being added to the reprocessing plant already there. In this way, both plants can service the prototype fast reactor on the site, and together, all three will constitute a completely self-contained nuclear power centre.

While the idea of the power park has many good points, it cannot be a general solution. The world trend is towards having a small number of large central reprocessing and fuel plants serving reactors everywhere, with fuel rods transported between them. The scheme advocated by Marshall[2] is to use the large central plants to give a quick 'turn around' of the plutonium *while its fuel rods are still highly radioactive*. This reprocessing might be done within a few months of the spent fuel leaving its reactor; and some radioactivity would be intentionally transferred to the new fuel rods, in the form of small amounts of radioactive substances not separated from the plutonium. The radioactive fuel rods would thus have to be transported in their special heavy steel flasks both from and to the reactors. To prepare for this method, new ways are being developed of reprocessing and making fuel rods completely remotely, by wholly automatic equipment. The fuel would be too radioactive to be handled manually even by people protected by standard shielding equipment.

In this method the plutonium would never become 'accessible' at any stage of the cycle. The only way to make nuclear explosive from it would be to construct a reprocessing plant at least as elaborate as those now being planned at centres such as Windscale. Such a plant could not be constructed clandestinely. It would require a large industrial site, with special access roads and service facilities, take years to build and cost around £1,000m.

For the 'quick turn around' scheme to succeed there would have to be reactors readily available to accept the new fuel elements as soon as these are made. This might become possible in about 50 years time, if FBRs are adopted at an early date as the main new reactors for the early twenty-first century. In the meantime, we have to deal with the present state of affairs in which our thermal reactors are producing plutonium—in spent fuel rods—that is unlikely to be converted into new fuel for some years yet. As emphasised by Marshall[2], interim measures are therefore needed, to avoid a temporary danger during the next fifty years from accessible plutonium accumulated at various reactor sites and fuel stores around the world. One idea for dealing with this is to make this plutonium up fairly quickly into new fuel rods for *thermal* reactors, perhaps irradiating them briefly before they leave the fuel plant so as to render them too radioactive to be handled by ordinary means.

International discussions

The danger of civil plutonium being diverted into bombs led President Carter to suggest, in 1977, that countries should re-examine from this point of view their plans for civil nuclear power. In response to this, a large international study, the *International Nuclear Fuel Cycle Evaluation* (INFCE), involving 66 countries, was held from 1977 to 1980. It was reckoned that the non-communist countries already have well over 20 tons of civil plutonium, and that these stocks will rise to nearly 150 tons during the 1980s. While most of this plutonium is expected to end up as fast reactor fuel, the INFCE study estimated that there would still be some 100 tons in store by the year 2,000.

The original view of the US authorities was that countries should agree to forego separating plutonium from spent reactor fuel; but the throw-away cycle ran into opposition, particularly from the Europeans and Japanese, partly on the grounds that it would waste the immense potential of uranium−238, and partly on the basis of technical arguments of the type outlined above.

The INFCE study came to the view that the separation of

plutonium, for the purpose of reactor fuel, had to be accepted as a means of extending energy supplies. The most promising idea to emerge was that all stocks of civil plutonium should be 'banked' at a small number of internationally controlled major centres, such as might be arranged at Windscale. The plutonium would be taken into custody there, probably under the control or supervision of the International Atomic Energy Agency (IAEA) and would not be released from this control except by the authority of the international custodian, who would require to be satisfied that it was intended for genuine use as civil reactor fuel.

References

1 *Sixth report of the Royal Commission on Environmental Pollution*, Chairman: Sir Brian (now Lord) Flowers, Command 6618, London, HMSO, September 1976.
2 W. Marshall, *Graham Young Memorial Lecture*, University of Glasgow 1978; *Atom* 258, 78, April 1978; *Atom*, 282, 88, April 1980.

16

Nuclear power and the nuclear powers

The problems of proliferation

It is ironic that the same word, *power*, can signify either electrical power or political/military power, for these two meanings converge in a real and disturbing sense when the power is nuclear. Electricity and bombs; how do we keep these two nuclear applications apart? As we have seen, formidable technical barriers separate them for terrorists. But national governments have vastly greater resources—scientific, industrial and economic—to overcome these barriers. Any sufficiently determined government can acquire atomic bombs, if it wishes. The fear is that, over the course of time, many and varied governments—including some that are aggressive, beleaguered, extremist, desperate or unstable—may get their own bombs, and sooner or later start using them. This is the general problem of *proliferation*, the spreading of nuclear weapons amongst more and more countries.

It is a general problem, because it would still exist even if there were no nuclear electrical power. A government does not need a civil nuclear plant, or even plutonium, in order to make atomic bombs. Nevertheless, a civil nuclear programme can clearly be of help to a government which intends to make bombs. It provides expertise in a nearby, though different, area of nuclear technology: it provides a source of plutonium; and it may provide a 'cover' or 'smokescreen' for a clandestine military project. This blurring of the boundaries between the two kinds of nuclear power—electrical and political/military—raises one of the central questions of proliferation: how to expand civil nuclear power throughout the world without fostering the spread of nuclear weapons.

Some comfort may be drawn from the fact that the above fear has not so far been justified by events. The bomb has not spread to many countries; and the existing nuclear powers have, since 1945, refrained from using it. Whether its possession in the hands of many small countries would produce a similar degree of responsibility and extreme caution is perhaps open to doubt. Nevertheless, it is an encouraging fact that even now, over one-third of a century after the bombs on

Japan, there are still only six overt nuclear powers: USA, USSR, UK, France, China and India. A few others, e.g. South Africa, Israel, Pakistan, are believed by many people to be on the brink. There may of course be still more, for it is a secret business.

Why have the numbers remained small? Partly of course because it is extremely difficult, even for an industrial country, to make an effective atomic bomb. The Indian government described as 'difficult' the task of producing its 1974 atomic explosion—which it did not regard as a weapon test. In every case, the project has taken several years and been extremely costly, even for a national treasury. But technical difficulty cannot be the only reason. Many industrial countries are clearly strong enough for the task. Countries such as Canada have very advanced civil nuclear programmes yet have not made bombs. In these countries there is clearly a *deliberate forbearance*, a voluntary political decision to forego nuclear weapons.

International organisations and treaties

This spirit of forbearance is formally recognised by the widespread acceptance of various international organisations and treaties. The International Atomic Energy Agency (IAEA) was set up in 1956 to foster the peaceful development of atomic energy. It has become the main international agency for monitoring this development, and for applying and checking safeguards against its diversion from civil to military applications. A key step was taken in 1968 with the *Nuclear Non-Proliferation Treaty* (NPT), which aimed to curb the spread of nuclear weapons while at the same time encouraging the spread of peaceful atomic energy. Over 100 countries now observe the treaty but, of the five nuclear-weapons states, only three (USA, USSR, UK) have ratified it. France, however, has said that she will act as if she were a party to the treaty; and China is thought likely to behave similarly.

The obligations on those who have ratified the treaty are, in the case of nuclear-weapons states, not to transfer nuclear weapons or their technology to non-nuclear-weapons states, but to encourage the development of peaceful atomic energy; and, in the case of non-nuclear-weapons states, not to make or acquire nuclear weapons, but to accept the controls and safeguards provided by the IAEA to prevent civil fissile material being diverted to non-peaceful purposes. The USA and UK, although not required to do so, have voluntarily accepted the application of these IAEA safeguards to their own civil nuclear industries. The IAEA monitors the observance of the NPT, and its safeguards involve the inspection of nuclear sites and the keeping of quantitative records of the production, movement and use of fissile materials, in order to detect at an early stage any large-scale diversion out of the civil nuclear economy. In Europe the signatories of the EURATOM Treaty, including the UK, also observe a similar set of safeguards.

depth at which elimination of a surface crack by simply grinding it out could be reasonably entertained. Beyond that depth (as well as in the case of all cracks deep inside the material) the vastly more difficult processes of re-welding and heat-treating deeply ground-out defective regions—all remotely in an operational vessel—have to be envisaged. This problem clearly weighed heavily with the French in their difficult recent decision to operate some of their PWRs, even though ¼ inch cracks had been discovered in them.

In the light of all this, it may be asked what steps are needed to ensure the safety of such vessels against sudden fracture. The following would all seem to be essential:

1 Apply rigorously all recommendations (e.g. as given in the Marshall Report, referred to below) for the manufacture, operation and inspection of the vessels.

2 Improve the ultrasonic technique and procedure to the level at which *in routine practice* it detects ¼ cracks with fair probability and 1 inch cracks with very high probability.

3 Develop methods for repairing cracks remotely in thick radio-active steel without impairing the mechanical properties of the material.

4 Repair by these methods all cracks deeper than ¼ inch.

References

1 W. Marshall, *An assessment of the integrity of PWR pressure vessels*, UKAEA, 1 October 1976.

2 *Plate Inspection Programme*, Nuclear Energy Agency Report, OECD, 1979.

These political agreements were made in the relatively stable conditions of the 1950s and 60s, when there was a fair chance of their being upheld and proliferation resisted. In fact, within their limits they have been successful. No country that is a party to the NPT has openly breached it, and the IAEA believes that none of these countries has clandestinely breached it, either. But the position is now growing more difficult. The world has become much less stable and orderly. Several advanced industrial nations are now able to supply nuclear equipment; and their commercial rivalry as well as political pressures may incline them to go beyond the NPT limits in exporting items that could be useful to bomb makers. The NPT was originally targeted mainly at those few highly industrialised countries who were beginning to develop large civil nuclear industries, whereas many other countries particularly in the Third World were not fully involved in it. The result today is that a number of countries who are not obliged to observe the NPT—some of whom are in strategically vulnerable positions or are politically aggressive—have begun to acquire the kinds of technology and facilities needed for bomb making. The old safeguards of the NPT and the IAEA are no longer sufficient for today's conditions. Something more is needed.

Proliferation from civil nuclear power

Are the two aims of the NPT incompatible: to resist the spread of nuclear weapons, and to encourage the spread of peaceful atomic energy? In one respect at least they probably are incompatible. The use of nuclear explosives for large civil engineering operations is so indistinguishable from bomb testing that the world ought to agree to forego this particular 'peaceful' use of atomic energy, which is in any case of only minor economic value. But nuclear electric power is a different matter altogether.

A civil power reactor is neither *necessary* nor *sufficient* for making nuclear explosive. It is not necessary because there are other methods, especially the isotopic separation of uranium−235 from natural uranium. The Hiroshima bomb was made this way, as was also the first Chinese bomb. Even for the plutonium bomb, however, a civil power reactor is not necessary. The original nuclear powers made their plutonium bombs using special military production reactors, which are far simpler and cheaper than civil power reactors. India obtained the plutonium for its 1974 explosion from a research reactor. A civil power reactor, or indeed any reactor, is of course not sufficient for making nuclear explosive, because it has to be supplemented by a reprocessing plant to obtain the plutonium in concentrated form.

The technical problems of proliferation from civil nuclear power thus centre around, not the power unit itself, but the ancillary plant, the *isotope separators* which may be needed to provide enriched reactor fuel but which can also be used for making uranium−235 explosive, and the *reprocessing plant* which may be needed for extracting plutonium fuel for the power reactor, but which can also be used for making plutonium explosive. This is why the recent efforts to strengthen the safeguards against proliferation, as in INFCE, have been focussed on the civil nuclear fuel cycle.

Apart from the NPT and IAEA safeguards, the two traditional methods that have been used to try to prevent the spread of nuclear weapons from civil nuclear activities have been *denial* and *inducement*. The policy of denial, or the threat of denial, has meant withholding critical nuclear knowledge or materials from other countries, particularly those suspected of wanting to make bombs. Knowledge of how to separate uranium isotopes, especially by the gas diffusion method, has been kept extremely secret. In addition, enriched nuclear reactor fuel has been withheld from countries who have not accepted safeguards against its diversion into weapons. But denial simply fails, except as a temporary measure. Indeed it could be counterproductive, by hardening a country's determination to equip itself fully, and to make itself completely self-sufficient and independent in all aspects of nuclear technology. It is likely that the invention and spread among several countries of new ways to separate uranium isotopes is due directly to the embargo placed upon the release of information about the original method.

The policy of *inducement* aims to make it unnecessary or economically unattractive for non-nuclear-weapon countries to set up their own separation or reprocessing plants. Certainly, a country which is genuinely interested only in nuclear electricity production basically needs only the nuclear power reactors themselves. It can buy its enriched fuel from other, more completely equipped, countries and also ship its spent fuel rods back to them for reprocessing. The expense and effort of building and running its own separation and reprocessing plants are then avoided. Moreover, the supply of fuel and removal of spent fuel can be underwritten by firm long-term agreements under favourable economic terms.

The trouble with this arrangement is its dependence on the stability of such international agreements, and on continuing international goodwill towards the recipient country. How can such a country be sure that, if a world shortage of uranium develops, or if there is a major political upheaval in its supplier country, its nuclear fuel supplies and removals will not be halted by external action? Or that it will never, despite precedents, be ostracised in the United Nations and strong pressure applied there to deny it these nuclear facilities?

It is clear, therefore, that the need for the security of its civil and economic activities ultimately points a country with civil nuclear power in the same direction as is pointed by its (believed) need for military security—towards complete nuclear independence and self-sufficiency, i.e. towards its own separation and reprocessing plants. This is perhaps the one really hard objection to civil nuclear energy:

that there is no technical way of spreading peaceful atomic energy without stimulating the spread of ancillary technologies that could also be used for producing nuclear explosives. The first responsibility of a national government is to provide for the security of its own people in every sense—economic, social, political, military—in an uncertain and often threatening world. If such a government sets out with real determination to acquire a complete range of nuclear facilities, the most that anyone outside can do is to slow the acquisition processes down. Nothing can stop the country going ahead with its plans, so long as the determination persists. If it believes it needs military security, through its own atomic bombs, then not even cutting it off completely from all civil nuclear power could prevent it from acquiring such bombs. Civil nuclear power can be an aid to atomic bomb power, but is not essential to it. The problem of proliferation is in the last analysis a problem of political intentions, which will continue to exist whether there is civil nuclear power or not. As a political problem, it calls for a political solution.

Steps towards a solution

On the overall problem of proliferation, one important step forward would be to set up and gain world-wide acceptance of a *Comprehensive Test Ban Treaty* which would forbid **all** testing of nuclear weapons (and also forbid the testing and use of 'peaceful' nuclear explosions). No country could feel confident in the military or political value of its nuclear weapons if these had never been tested. Good methods for detecting nuclear explosions have now been developed, and international economic and political sanctions could be brought to bear on transgressors.

More generally, however, the overriding need is to remove the causes of proliferation, which are to be found in the various political conditions and attitudes of different countries. It is understandable that a heavily beleaguered country should try to grasp every apparent means of security that it can, even to the extent of acquiring its own nuclear weapons. The main direction for world nuclear security must therefore be towards the reinvigoration and renewal of the high purposes for which the United Nations was originally set up and which have become so bedraggled in recent years.

On the specific problem of proliferation from civil nuclear programmes, it needs to be clearly recognised that even a total decoupling of civil and military technologies cannot stop proliferation, if the basic causes of this are not removed. If these causes continue, then proliferation will continue, irrespective of civil nuclear power. If they are removed, then civil nuclear power no longer carries the fear of proliferation. The purpose of efforts to decouple civil and military nuclear power is therefore essentially the same as that of trying to achieve a comprehensive test ban treaty. It is to make proliferation as technically difficult and unattractive as possible, as a secondary strategy to dissuade undecided countries, so complementing the primary strategy which is to relax the general political, economic and social driving forces for proliferation.

The only realistic way to this decoupling is through a widening and strengthening of the NPT and the IAEA safeguards. The key steps here are to get the full adherence of all countries to the NPT: to increase the capacity of the IAEA to carry out its monitoring functions by means of frequent inspections of all nuclear plants; and to devise an unbreakable way of guaranteeing nuclear fuel supplies and fuel services to all countries which observe the NPT and IAEA safeguards. These supplies and services should be available on economic terms which are clearly better than these countries could obtain by setting up their own separation and reprocessing plants.

17

Nuclear safety in focus

The general public's view

It is time now to turn to the questions raised in the opening chapter. Why is nuclear safety such a big public issue? Are there real causes for worry? If so, what are they? Can they be removed? But if there are not such causes, why has nuclear safety been made such a matter of public concern? Are there other reasons for the campaigns to rouse public fears, and has nuclear safety been made a stalking horse for these? These are questions not only about the safety of civil nuclear power but even more about its public *acceptability*.

Although there have been intensive campaigns by anti-nuclear protesters, which have often skilfully gained good press publicity, and although there has been intense and understandable alarm at Harrisburg and the other towns near Three Mile Island, the general public nevertheless has on the whole continued to give qualified support to civil nuclear power. Listen to Members of Parliament's reports about the views of their constituents; follow the correspondence columns in the newspapers; or simply ask people whom one meets in everyday life; all these guides to public opinion point to the conclusion that nuclear energy is still broadly acceptable. More formally, there have been public surveys to test the general state of opinion. In 1977 the Journal *New Society*[1] reported that over two-thirds of a representative sample of people in Britain believed nuclear power stations to be reasonably safe; and that nearly as many as this would tolerate the building of one within ten miles of their homes.

Informal enquiries also quickly show that the aspect that matters most to the general public is safety against radiations which could be dangerous to health. A few people still think that a nuclear reactor could 'blow up like an atomic bomb'—a misapprehension which does little credit to either the pro-nuclear or anti-nuclear publicists. But the main fear is of the escape of radioactivity from nuclear plants. By contrast, the problem of proliferation of nuclear weapons from civil nuclear programmes seems to have made less impression on the public mind, at least in Britain. What people tend to say about this is that if atomic bombs do ever fall on Britain they will have come from Russia, having been made there in thousands in large military establishments, and not from a Third World country where they were made in ones and twos, surreptitiously, from a civil programme.

Anti-nuclear views

It is difficult to bring the views of the anti-nuclear protesters into a single focus because they are so diverse and changeable. Whenever a prepared refutation of one of the protesters' objections is put forward, they tend to respond by saying that *this* was not their real objection, which was *that*, instead. It must be frustrating for the nuclear industry to try to conduct a rational debate against such hit-and-run opponents. Of course, the anti-nuclear groups themselves are very heterogeneous, with a wide range of motives for opposing civil nuclear power, and an equally wide range of opinions on what are the important objections.

For some, the main reason is the environmental hazard, which primarily means the release of **radioactivity**, whether from normal operations, or accidents, or nuclear waste. For example, Dr Stewart[2] believes that the levels of radiation released in **normal operations** are too high, and seriously endanger the nuclear workers themselves; whereas Professor Bryce-Smith and colleagues[3] have said that the **long-term storage of nuclear waste** is the real problem. This view is shared by Professor Alfvén[4], although he also regards **proliferation**, through a coupling of civil nuclear power to nuclear weapons production, as no less important. Barnaby[5] goes beyond this by saying that proliferation and the diversion of plutonium are more important than the disposal of radioactive waste or reactor accidents, a view which Patterson[6] appears to share, with his description of the FBR and plutonium fuel as forming an 'atom bomb economy'. By contrast, Ryle[7] has said that the most serious dangers to the public are not nuclear explosions but **radioactivity releases from reactor accidents and nuclear waste**.

All these objections have been discussed in previous chapters. But for some nuclear objectors the radioactive hazards take second place to **political** objections, ranging from objections to heavy industry and possible threats to civil liberties all the way to broad anti-Western attitudes. For example, Morgan-Grenville[8] has said that the main arguments are not against the safety of nuclear technology but against the **infrastructure** needed to support a State which is reliant upon nuclear technology; and Cotgrove[9] has similarly observed that the rooted objections of anti-nuclear environmentalists are not to nuclear safety as such but to **large, remote, impersonal bureaucracies**. French nuclear protesters have described this more brutally, but revealingly, as *electro-fascism*, i.e. the formation of a highly centralised, heavily industrialised state with massive police and para-military forces[10]. For Sieghart[11] also, the **threat to civil liberties** is more serious than the technological problems of nuclear energy. And, as regards proliferation, some environmentalists regard the diversion of plutonium and the problems of Patterson's 'atom bomb economy' as less important than the **spread of uranium enrichment technology**[12]. Then again, Goldsmith and others have asserted that it 'is not the bomb which is disturbing about nuclear power, it is rather the irrevocable social, environmental and political implications of pursuing a policy of aimless growth based on expensive energy'[13].

What are we to make of these objections, which point in all directions and so often one against another? Is it *really* safety that worries the objectors? If it is, then a remarkable conclusion must follow. For the USSR has one of the largest civil nuclear power programmes and also exports power reactors to other countries, yet it attracts hardly a word of anti-nuclear protest, either from within its own borders or from the vociferous groups in the west. The safety of *some* civil nuclear plants, at least, is evidently not a worry to the protesters.

A much more convincing interpretation is that the real driving force behind the anti-nuclear movement is socio-political. It is the manifestation of a more general aversion to modern Western society, to massive industrialisation, high technology, central bureaucracy and security forces, and to free enterprise and economic growth. Certainly, this seems to be the most consistent thread running through the protesters' many views, albeit one that itself varies over a wide range from the civilised 'small is beautiful' arguments of some environmentalists to the violence of some mass demonstrations at nuclear plants. Extremist politics has become clearly connected with some parts of the anti-nuclear movement, as for example in the demonstrations against uranium mining in Australia, the clashes at nuclear sites in France and Germany and the march against a nuclear reactor project at Torness, in Scotland. Political extremist groups carry banners into the more violent confrontations, which sometimes give the impression of being five-finger exercises for revolutionists.

Despite all the confusion and contradictions of the protesters' various statements, and the sound and fury of the demonstrations and marches, it is usually not difficult to recognise whether safety or politics is the ultimate driving force. True concern with safety, pure and simple, produces an outlook very much like that of the Flowers Report[14]—i.e. a qualified acceptance of the broad feasibility of safe nuclear power; a discrimination between different kinds of nuclear developments, praising some as more safe, criticising others as less safe; and a general welcoming of all steps that clearly enhance safety. Political objection produces an uncompromising and more extremist outlook, a total rejection of all (western) nuclear power, a refusal to discriminate except in the entirely negative terms of saying that 'system Y is even worse than system X' in case one might be accused of actually favouring a nuclear system such as X. Every conceivable objection is called up, not only safety, but also economic ('it is too expensive'), social ('it isn't needed, will be too late anyway, and couldn't meet the needs') and resources ('there isn't enough uranium'). For the politic-ally-motivated protester there is no redeeming feature to be admitted anywhere in nuclear energy. If such a comprehensive portfolio of faults were valid, no civil nuclear project could possibly ever have gone forward, for not even the most illiterate engineer, most grasping indus-trialist, most non-numerate public servant and most starry-eyed Minister of Energy could have overlooked or ignored such a damning list of minuses, without a single relieving plus.

The view from this book

Ultimately, therefore, we have to make up our own minds, from all that has gone before in the previous chapters.

Some of the fears that have been expressed about the safety of civil nuclear power are clearly not justified. Thus, a nuclear reactor cannot explode as an atomic bomb because its fissile material is too diluted with non-fissile and neutron-absorbing uranium—238—so much so in a thermal reactor that the neutrons have to become thermalised in a moderator before they can continue the chain reaction (Chapter 2).

For estimating the **health effects** of nuclear radiation the established method of linear extrapolation, from high doses to low, provides a reliable figure for the upper limit to the damage that might be caused by low doses. This is confirmed by actual observations, which do not show any detectable health effects except where, as in the case of the natural radiations at Kerala, the dose becomes large enough for the linear extrapolation method to warn of the chance of such effects (Chapters 3 and 4).

The health hazard due to radioactive releases from **normal civil nuclear activities** and **low-level wastes** is extremely small. The average person receives much less radiation from these sources than from natural radiation, or from the additional natural radiation due to living on granite, or from medical X-rays, or from burning coal, or from various other activities such as watching television, flying in jet air-craft, etc. (none of which produces perceptible medical effects). The amounts of radioactivity permitted to be released in civil nuclear operations are so low that even abnormally exposed people and workers in the nuclear plants receive doses well inside the limits set by the International Commission on Radiological Protection (Chapters 4, 5 and 6). As regards the future, the method of storing highly active waste in glass blocks, buried deeply underground in geologically stable and dry sites, offers virtually certain protection for some thousands of years, even though the radioactivity of these deposits will decay to less than that of the original uranium ore, from which they came, after about 1,000 years (Chapter 13).

Sweeping generalisations about safety from **accidents** at nuclear plants are worthless. Statements such as 'all reactors are dangerous' or that 'nuclear energy is safe' are propaganda, not safety assessments.

We would never dream of making such simplistic remarks about, say, all vehicles, or ball games, or electricity in the home. Each particular case has to be taken on its own merits and separately argued. Some are more safe than others, some are safe in some conditions, dangerous in others. It is the same with nuclear plants. Different types have different problems and must be separately analysed. There is a lot of combustible material in gas-graphite reactors and sodium-cooled fast breeder reactors, but not in water reactors. The coolant is necessarily under high pressure in thermal power reactors, contained in a highly-stressed pressure vessel and circuit, but not in LMFBRs. If a depressurisation accident occurs in a thermal reactor, the coolant can flash from water to steam in a water reactor but not in a gas-cooled one. Some water reactors use multiple pressure tubes, others use a single large pressure vessel. Interruption of the coolant flow, for example by a blockage formed in a fuel channel, is more serious in a high-intensity than in a low-intensity reactor. All these and many other differences have to be separately examined and assessed, before any worthwhile statements about accident safety can be attempted. Such analyses bring out various points which we have outlined in Chapters 7 to 12 above. The natural safety features of the advanced gas-cooled reactor are one such example; the enclosure of water and sodium cooled reactors in strong containment buildings is another.

Some general points also emerge from the detailed analysis. There is the importance of having **natural** safety, as far as possible; for example, oxide reactor fuel of very high melting point, negative temperature coefficient of nuclear reactivity, coolant which cannot change its physical state in a depressurisation accident or a temperature excursion, coolant which can function effectively by natural circulation, pressure vessels and circuits which can fail only gradually, not suddenly; and as a last resort there is the natural public safety which comes from remote siting. But not all these natural safety features are of course achievable in particular systems and some **engineered** safety cannot be avoided. The general principles here are obviously to use very high standards of design, construction, inspection and operation —although these are always to some extent vulnerable to human limitations—and to rely on automatic, multiple, independently acting devices for all the important safety systems. In addition, the aim is to provide a defence in depth, as far as possible, so that at least two quite different and wholly independent major things have to go wrong before there can be a serious accident.

These precautions are impressive, but all engineered safety ultimately depends upon the human qualities of those who design, build, test and run the plant. The accident at Three Mile Island revealed important weaknesses in the arrangements for relating the human operators to the reactor's control and emergency systems. A development in reactor technology generally, towards total and foolproof automation of all the controls under both normal and emergency conditions, is inevitable, but it will exacerbate the problem of deciding the functions and powers of the control room staffs (Chapter 12). Much more study of this is needed. This problem is of course not unique to the nuclear industry. The flight deck crews of large civil aircraft are similarly placed and the air transport industry already has a great deal of useful experience to offer.

What can we finally conclude about safety from accidents? The amount of radioactivity which builds up inside a nuclear plant is certainly large and hence potentially very dangerous. But so many different kinds of safety barriers can be built round this radioactivity that the risk of its escaping to the general public can be brought down almost to zero. This means that civil nuclear power *can* in principle be safe. The question of the extent to which it *will* be safe in practice depends on much more detailed considerations, on the choices of particular types of plant and processes, and on the formulation of and insistence upon rigorous standards. Accidents will of course always happen. But it is entirely within reach of present capabilities to ensure that bad accidents, which produce public casualties, will occur *much more rarely* than equally bad accidents in other walks of life that are already publicly tolerated as bearable in relation to the benefits provided (Chapter 11).

Finally, there are the problems of the *proliferation* of nuclear weapons and the diversion of dangerous materials from civil nuclear power programmes (Chapters 14 to 16). While proliferation is undoubtedly a major world problem, it is to a large extent independent of civil nuclear power. A total ban on civil nuclear power would not eliminate the proliferation problem because many other and technically better routes to the acquisition of nuclear weapons exist. We have seen that various steps can be taken to make civil nuclear power an extremely difficult and unattractive route for a country which intends to acquire nuclear weapons and an almost impossible route for a terrorist organisation. Such actions will not of course dispose of the general proliferation problem, which needs a political solution at the international level, but they can assure that civil nuclear power will not make it worse.

Conclusion

Life began on earth about 3,500 million years ago. The first organisms lived off a rich store of fossil energy, a soup of energy-rich molecules in the oceans. They thrived and multiplied until this store was nearly all consumed. Faced by this challenge, life then made its greatest discovery, photosynthesis, which opened up an entirely new access to a different energy source. The organisms could live directly off sunlight and so they became independent of fossil energy. This 'age of solar energy' lasted unchallenged for about 2,000 million years, until life discovered another store of fossil energy, a few hundred years ago, in the form of coal and then also of oil and natural gas. History is now repeating itself and life is challenged once more by the exhaustion of stocks of fossil energy. Yet again, life has made a great discovery, this time nuclear power, which can open up access to an entirely different energy source. This new source has its risks. But so had photosynthesis, which introduced a major poison—oxygen—into the early organisms. Modern life has the inestimable advantage of intelligence, which allows it to understand the hazards and think out steps to protect itself against them.

The long thrust of life, over the millenia, is inevitably towards any new energy source that will succour it. The next move into nuclear energy is inevitable. Life now expresses itself, through ourselves, consciously. We should not use our fears to try to turn the clock back but instead use our intelligence in order to enjoy the benefits of nuclear power safely.

References

1 *New Society*, 31 March 1977.
2 Alice Stewart, quoted in *The Observer*, 2 Oct. 1977.
3 D. Bryce-Smith *et al, The Guardian*, 7 January 1975.
4 Alfvén, quoted by D. Fishlock, *Financial Times*, 10 May 1977.
5 F. Barnaby, *New Scientist*, 29 May 1975.
6 Walter C. Patterson, *The Observer*, 25 July 1976.
7 Sir Martin Ryle, *The Daily Telegraph*, 28 December 1978.
8 G. Morgan-Grenville, *Financial Times*, 26 September 1978.
9 S. F. Cotgrove, *The Times*, 27 November 1978.
10 V. W. Leigh, *The Sunday Times*, 20 April 1975.
11 Paul Sieghart, *The Times*, 31 March 1977.
12 Quoted by D. Fishlock *Financial Times*, 10 May 1978.
13 E. Goldsmith *et al, The Times*, 14 February 1978.
14 *Sixth report of the Royal Commission on Environmental Pollution*, Chairman: Sir Brian (now Lord) Flowers, Command 6618, HMSO, September 1976.

Glossary of special terms

Actinides
A series of heavy chemical elements, including *uranium* and *plutonium*, most of which emit *alpha particles*.

Alpha particle
A helium−4 nucleus, consisting of two *protons* and two *neutrons*, emitted from a radioactive nucleus.

Atom
The smallest unit of a chemical element. It consists of a small, central *nucleus* surrounded by a 'planetary' system of one or more *electrons*, the negative electrical charges of which balance the positive charge due to *protons* in the nucleus. Most of the weight of an atom is in the nucleus. The diameter of an atom, about one hundred-millionth of an inch, is determined by the orbits of the electrons.

BEIR
Committee (US NAS-NRC) on Biological Effects of Ionising Radiation.

Beta particle
An *electron*, emitted by a radioactive nucleus. A positively charged beta particle is called a *positron* and is the 'anti-particle' of the electron.

Boron
A neutron-absorbing element used in reactor control rods.

Breeding
Transmutation of non-fissile nuclei into fissile nuclei, e.g. *uranium−238* into *plutonium*, usually by the absorption of *neutrons*.

Burn up
The consumption of the fissile component of nuclear fuel through fission produced by *neutron* irradiation in a nuclear reactor.

Can
A continuous envelope of cladding material in which nuclear fuel is sealed to protect it and to retain its fission products.

Centrifuge
A device for separating constituents of a mixture by centrifugal acceleration in a rapidly rotating vessel. In the gas centrifuge isotopes of *uranium* are separated while in the form of a gaseous compound (uranium hexafluoride).

Chain reaction
A reaction whose products set off further reactions of the same kind. The product which does

	this in a nuclear chain reaction is the *neutron*, produced from a fission reaction and able to set of a further fission reaction in another fissile nucleus.
China syndrome	An imagined accident in which reactor fuel greatly overheats and forms a molten pool which melts its way down, through the reactor vessel, through its containment, and on down into the earth below, 'heading (in the western world) for China'.
Cladding	See Can.
Comprehensive Test Ban Treaty	A hoped-for treaty which would ban all tests of nuclear weapons. Tests in the atmosphere and outer space were banned in 1963. Underground tests are not banned.
Control rods	Rods of a neutron-absorbing substance, usually boron in steel, which are lowered into a nuclear reactor to control the *reactivity* by stabilising the *chain reaction*.
Core	The central part of a fission reactor where the nuclear *chain reaction* takes place.
Criticality	The condition in a nuclear reactor where each *fission* leads to exactly one more fission and the population of neutrons remains constant. A nuclear chain reaction is *prompt critical* when this condition is achieved using *prompt neutrons* alone; and it is said to be *delayed critical* when *delayed neutrons* are also necessary for criticality.
Curie	The unit of *radioactivity*, equal to 37,000 million nuclear disintegrations per second. One gramme of radium-226 provides 1 curie. A *microcurie* is 1 millionth of a curie.
Decay heat	Heat produced by the nuclear disintegration of fission products, which continues even after the nuclear chain reaction has stopped.
Delayed neutron	See Neutron.
Deuterium	See Hydrogen.
Diffusion process	A method of enriching uranium with its fissile isotope, uranium-235, by passing uranium hexafluoride gas through a series of fine membranes. The different isotopes pass through these at slightly different rates.

DNA	Deoxyribonucleic acid, the long-chain molecule in chromosomes of biological cells, which is the carrier of genetic information.
ECCS	See Emergency core cooling system.
Electromagnetic waves	Oscillating electric and magnetic fields propagated through free space at the speed of light. Radio, radar infra-red, light and ultra-violet waves are all of this kind, as also are X-rays and gamma rays. They differ only in their frequencies (or wavelengths).
Electron	Lightweight, negatively charged particle which is a key constituent of all atomic and molecular matter. The *positron*, produced in some *beta* radiations, is identical except that it has a positive electrical charge.
Electron-volt	A small unit of energy equal to that which is acquired when an electron moves through an electric field of 1 volt. One atom is bound to another in a molecule with an energy of a few electron-volts. Nuclear particles in nuclei are bound together with energies of millions of electron-volts (1 MeV = 1 million electron-volts).
Emergency core cooling system	A reserve system for flooding a reactor core with coolant, should the main cooling system fail.
Enrichment	The raising of the fissile content of a material for nuclear fuel, usually by *diffusion* or *centrifuge* methods of *isotopic separation*.
EURATOM	European Atomic Energy Community.
Event tree analysis	A systematic procedure for analysing various faults in an engineering system by considering all combinations of success or failure in the operations of every component of the system.
Fast breeder reactor	A reactor in which, due to a high content of fissile material (usually plutonium), the nuclear chain reaction is sustained by *fast neutrons*; and in which new fuel is *bred* by the absorption, usually in uranium−238, of surplus neutrons.
Fast neutron	See Neutron.
Fission	The splitting of a nucleus such as that of uranium−235 into two slightly unequal *fission*

fragments, after absorbing a neutron. About 200 MeV of energy and 2 or 3 neutrons are also released in the fission process. The fission fragments become *fission products*, radioactive atoms of medium atomic weights.

Frequency of wave radiation

The number of oscillations per second in a wave motion. It is closely related to the energy of a unit *pulse* of the radiation. High-energy nuclear processes produce high-frequency *gamma* radiation.

Fuel cycle

The total process of preparing a nuclear fuel, using it in a reactor, removing the spent fuel, storing it, and then possibly *reprocessing* it to use some again in a recycled fuel. The 'once-through' or 'throw-away' cycles do not go beyond the stage of storing the spent fuel.

Fuel element

A *rod* or *pin* of fuel, in its *can*. Fuel elements are sometimes grouped in *bundles* and joined end-to-end in *stringers*.

Fusion

The uniting of two light nuclei, usually *isotopes* of hydrogen, to make one heavier one, usually helium, generally with a release of energy.

Gamma ray

A pulse of high-energy (e.g. 1 MeV) electro-magnetic radiation emitted from an atomic nucleus.

Gaseous diffusion

See Diffusion process.

Half-life

The time in which the number of nuclei of a particular type is reduced to one-half by spontaneous nuclear disintegration.

Heavy water

Water in which the hydrogen atoms all consist of *deuterium*. It is an excellent *moderator* substance. Ordinary water contains 1 part in 6,700 of heavy water.

Helium

The stable isotope, helium-4, of this chemical element has an alpha particle for its nucleus. Helium cooling is used in high-temperature gas-cooled reactors.

Hydrogen

The simplest and lightest atom, a single electron circulating round a nucleus containing a single proton. Two isotopic variants, *hydrogen-2* (*deuterium*) with a single neutron attached to the proton, and *hydrogen—3* (*tritium*) with two neutrons attached, are important in atomic energy.

IAEA   International Atomic Energy Agency.

ICRP   International Commission on Radiological Protection.

INFCE   International Nuclear Fuel Cycle Evaluation, an international study of non-proliferating fuel cycles, held from 1977 to 1980.

Ionisation   The conversion of an initially neutral atom into an electrically charged one, by losing or gaining an electron or electrons. The neutral atom becomes a *positive ion* when it loses electrons, or a *negative ion* when it gains electrons.

Isotopes   Nuclei of a given chemical element with different numbers of neutrons, e.g. hydrogen—1 (1 proton, no neutrons), hydrogen—2 (1 proton, 1 neutron) and hydrogen—3 (1 proton, 2 neutrons). Some important isotopes, with half-lives given, are as follows:
Americium—241 (433 years)
    ,,   —243 (7,370 years)
Argon—41 (1.8 hours)
Caesium—137 (30 years)
Carbon—14 (5,800 years)
Curium—242 (163 days)
Hydrogen—3 (tritium)(12 years)
Iodine—131 (8 days)
Krypton—85 (11 years)
Potassium—40 (1,300 million years)
Plutonium—239 (24,400 years)
    ,,   —240 (6,600 years)
Radon—222 (3.8 days)
Radium—226 (1,600 years)
Ruthenium—106 (1 year)
Strontium—90 (28 years)
Thorium—232 (14,000 million years)
Uranium—235 (700 million years)
    ,,   —238 (4,500 million years)
Xenon—133 (5 days)

Leak-before-break   When a crack grows in the wall of a boiler or pressure vessel, it may penetrate right through, thus allowing the contents to leak, before it has reached the critical size at which it can spread rapidly and break the vessel apart.

Linear hypothesis	The assumption that the biological effects of radiation extend, in unvarying proportionality with dose, over the whole range from very large to vanishingly small doses.
Man-rem	The sum of all rems of radiation accumulated by a given number of people. For example 10 rem to each of 10 people, or 1 rem to each of 100 people, would both count as 100 man-rem.
Maximum permissible body burden	The MPBB is the amount of a particular radioactive substance in the body of a radiation worker that would irradiate that person to the limit of the recommended standards.
Maximum permissible concentration	The MPC is the concentration of a particular radioactive substance in the air or drinking water that would cause someone exposed to it for 40 hours a week to be irradiated to the limit of the recommended standards.
Megawatt	A unit of power, mainly used in the electric supply industry, equal to 1 million watts. It could supply 1,000 one-kilowatt domestic electric heaters.
Melt-down	The melting and slumping down of overheated fuel rods in a serious reactor accident, generally leading to a large-scale release of radioactive substances into the coolant and possibly also to the *China syndrome*.
MeV	See Electron volt.
Microcurie	See Curie.
Moderator	A substance used in the core of a thermal reactor to slow down neutrons by allowing them to undergo, without absorption, a large number of 'billiard ball' collisions with the nuclei of the substance, so reducing their motion to that of ordinary heat motion at the temperature of the moderator. The main moderator substances are heavy water, light water and graphite.
Mutation	A change in the DNA genetic molecule which gives heritable variation when transmitted to offspring.
Neutron	Elementary particle similar to the *proton* but electrically uncharged, which exists in atomic

nuclei. Fission releases 2 or 3 *fast* neutrons at speeds of about 10,000 miles a second. The *prompt* neutrons are released immediately. A small number of *delayed* neutrons appear later. Fast neutrons are slowed down in a moderator to become *thermal* neutrons, at speeds of about 1 mile a second.

NII — Nuclear Installations Inspectorate (UK).

NPT — Nuclear Non-Proliferation Treaty.

NRC — Nuclear Regulatory Commission (USA).

NRPB — National Radiological Protection Board (UK).

Nuclear waste — Unwanted radioactive materials produced from nuclear reactors and reprocessing plant.

Nucleic acids — Unit molecules of the genetic code, strung together in long chains, in DNA.

Plutonium — A fissile element produced by transmutation of uranium−238 after absorbing a neutron. It exists in two main forms, plutonium−239 and plutonium−240. Used in fast reactor fuel.

Plutonium economy — The possible large-scale production of and international trading in plutonium reactor fuel, due to the widespread growth in nuclear power and fuel reprocessing

Power reactor — A nuclear reactor designed and used for the purpose of producing electrical power. To be distinguished from military plutonium-producing reactors and research reactors.

Proliferation — The acquisition by more countries of nuclear weapons and the means to produce them.

Prompt critical — See Criticality.

Prompt neutron — See Neutron.

Proton — The nucleus of the lightest *isotope* of hydrogen. A stable and positively charged particle, 1,840 times heavier than an electron, present in all nuclei. The chemical species of an atom is determined by the number of protons in its nucleus.

Pulse of radiation — Electromagnetic waves exist in unit pulses, known as *quanta* or *photons*. The energy of a quantum always bears a fixed relation to the frequency. High-frequency quanta such as gamma pulses have high energies, and vice versa.

Rad
A unit of absorbed radiation, that deposits 100 ergs of energy in 1 gramme of tissue.

Radiation sickness
Illness developed quickly after a heavy dose of radiation. To be contrasted with long-term effects (cancer and genetic).

Radioactivity
Transformations in unstable nuclei, resulting in the emission of nuclear particles and gamma radiation.

Radium
The most important naturally occurring radio-active element. Widely distributed in small amounts. Used in radiotherapy.

Radon
A radioactive gas produced naturally by the decay of radium, thorium and other actinides. Widely distributed in small amounts; and, in unventilated spaces, a hazard to health.

Reactivity
A measure of the extent to which the nuclear conditions in a reactor deviate from the *delayed critical* state.

Rem
That dose of radiation which produces biological effects in mankind equivalent to 1 rad of X-rays. It is related to the *rad* by the *quality factor* of the radiation.

Reprocessing
The chemical separation of spent nuclear fuel into uranium, plutonium and radioactive waste.

Safety rods
Fail-safe neutron-absorbing shut-down rods for sudden insertion into a reactor during an emergency. Also known as *scram* rods.

Shut-down rods
Neutron-absorbing control rods which, when inserted into a reactor, shut down the chain reaction.

Separation
The process of *enriching* uranium in the content of its fissile isotope, uranium−235, by removing some or all of the 238 isotope. The two main methods used are *diffusion* and *centrifuging*.

Temperature coefficient
The effect of temperature on the intensity of the nuclear reaction in a reactor, which may be positive or negative. A negative coefficient produces a stable reaction when any incipient temperature rise removes all the excess reactivity responsible for that temperature rise.

Thermal neutron	See Neutron.
Thermal reactor	A reactor in which the nuclear chain reaction is maintained by thermal neutrons, slowed down in a *moderator*.
Thermonuclear reaction	The fusing together, at very high temperatures, of light nuclei to form heavier nuclei, e.g. hydrogen into helium.
Transmutation	The conversion of an atomic nucleus into a different type of nucleus by the absorption or emission of a nuclear particle.
Toxic potential	The amount of water in which a given quantity of a radioactive substance would have to be dissolved in order to reduce the concentration to the permissible level for drinking water.
Tritium	See Hydrogen.
Ultrasonic inspection	A method of detecting cracks, usually inside thick steel used for boilers and pressure vessels, by the reflection of high-frequency sound waves (echo sounding) from discontinuities in the material.
UNSCEAR	United Nations Scientific Committee on the Effects of Atomic Radiation.
Uranium	The heaviest naturally occurring chemical element, consisting mainly of uranium-238 together with 0.7% of the fissile isotope, uranium-235 and traces of radioactive decay products. In *enriched* uranium for reactors the proportion of uranium-235 is increased to a few percent.
Void coefficient	The effect of a void, e.g. a vapour bubble in a liquid moderator or coolant, upon the intensity of the nuclear reaction in a reactor. May be positive or negative. See Temperature Coefficient.
WASH-1400	Report of the Reactor Safety Study (N. C. Rasmussen), US Nuclear Regulatory Commission, October 1975.
Waste	See Nuclear waste.
X-ray	High frequency electromagnetic radiation of the same type as gamma radiation but produced by processes outside the atomic nucleus.

Index